Softly molded, almost feminine lines of the 1961 250 short-wheelbase
berlinetta belie its fantastic performance. *Pininfarina*

Motorbooks International Illustrated Buyer's Guide Series

Illustrated

FERRARI
BUYER'S ★ GUIDE™

Fourth Edition

Dean Batchelor
Revised and Updated by Randy Leffingwell

This Fourth Edition published in 1996 by Motorbooks International Publishers & Wholesalers, PO Box 2, 729 Prospect Avenue, Osceola, WI 54020 USA

Motorbooks International books are also available at discounts in bulk quantity for industrial or sales-promotional use. For details write to Special Sales Manager at the Publisher's address

Library of Congress Cataloging-in-Publication Data Available

ISBN 0-7603-0243-X

On the front cover: Though out of production since 1992, the F40 is still one of the most advanced and fantastic cars in the world. *Randy Leffingwell*

On the back cover: Top: Ferrari's incredible 1995 F50. A mere 349 examples were built of this Formula One-based super car. *Ferrari North America* Bottom: The F50's 65-degree V-12 pumps out 513 horsepower propelling the car to a top speed of 202 miles per hour. *Ferrari North America*

Printed in the United States of America

Contents

Credits and Acknowledgments

I want to express my sincere and grateful thanks to those who contributed time, photos, or information to aid the creation of this book.

Karl Dedolph
Ed Niles
Bill Rudd
Pininfarina
Jonathan Thompson
Michael Baranowski, *Petersen's Kit Car magazine Automotive Investment Newsletter,* Vol. 1, No. 10—Stan Nowak
Ferrari Market Letter—Gerald Roush
Ferrari Cars 1962-1966—Brooklands Books
Ferrari Cars 1966-1969—Brooklands Books
Ferrari: The Sports & Gran Turismo Cars—Fitzgerald, Merritt & Thompson
Road & Track library
The Ferrari Legend: The Road Cars—Antoine Prunet
The Berlinetta Lusso—Kurt Miska
The Spyder California—George Carrick
The Ferrari Legend: 250 GT Competition—Jess G. Pourret
The Ferrari 365 GTB/4 Daytona—Pat Braden and Gerald Roush
Cavallino—John W. Barnes, Jr.

Dean Batchelor

Following in footsteps so deep as those Dean Batchelor imbedded into automotive literature is a daunting task. As Dean did with his first three editions of this book, I too want to express my sincere thanks to those who contributed time, photos, information, or philosophy to aid in the continuation of this guide.

First and foremost I thank Dean, who inspired and encouraged me to do my first book and whose experience and advice have directed my own path.

I am grateful to Giampaolo Letta, public relations manager, Ferrari North America, Englewood Cliffs, New Jersey, for his help in updating this book. I also wish to express my appreciation and gratitude to John Amette, technical zone manager, Ferrari North America, Cyprus, California, for his invaluable assistance.

Further thanks for their efforts are due to Raoul "Sonny" Balcaen, Los Angeles, California; John Barnes, Boca Raton, Florida; Allen Bishop, Galloway Enterprises, Pacific Palisades, California; George Carrick, Symbolic Motor Car Company, La Jolla, California; John Clinard, Irvine, California; Pat Current, administrator, Ferrari Club of America, Silver Springs, Maryland; Robert Hoye, *Puantum Research*, Vancouver, British Columbia; Mike Lynch, Mill Valley, California; Steve Sailors, Huntington Beach, California; and Jim Sitz, Bonsall, California.

Randy Leffingwell

Introduction

When Dean Batchelor wrote the first edition of *Illustrated Ferrari Buyer's Guide* in the winter of 1980–81, it was a fairly simple matter to locate and buy a Ferrari. Prices were already high for some models, but a Ferrari V-12 in pretty good shape could be obtained for less than $15,000. For that price it might need some work before you could drive it with any degree of reliability, and it would certainly need work before it could be shown at a Concours d'Elegance or driven in competition, but prices were reasonable.

On that basis, it was also easy to assign a value rating to each of the models discussed in this book. Even though prices had already started to escalate, they were moving upward at an almost predictable rate.

Since then, a combination of events caused Ferrari prices to increase as much as ten times (and even more in some instances) their 1980 value: the decreased value of the dollar versus the yen, pound, mark, lira, kronor, as well as the instability of the stock market, brought investor and speculator attention to Ferraris as a new collectible. This shot prices completely out of the reach of genuine enthusiasts.

Robert Hoye, publisher of *Quantum Research*, an institutional investment advisory newsletter out of Vancouver, British Columbia, has investigated consumer price indices all the way back to 1280 A.D. The pattern he has observed tracks something like 30-year-long periods of dynamic economic expansion that always ends with a 10-year frenzy of high speculative investment including such commodities as zinc and copper, paintings, and cars. The demise of tangible investments in 1920 was followed by the crash of the stock market in 1929. This happened again in 1980 and 1989 when car prices, driven up by "new kids on the block" descended like a burst balloon.

Hoye had completed his research in 1976 and he sat back and waited for history to repeat itself. He chose to track not only traditional speculative commodities but he also added to his chart the Ferrari 275GTB4. He sought a car with enough production (280) to be a valid sample but also enough interest to have a level of appeal that could honestly relate its value to other, rarer models such as the 250 GTO (with only 36 produced). Sales and trades of 275GTB4s happened frequently enough to accurately track its price over time.

Fueled by such high visibility events as Steve Earle's Monterey Historic Automobile Races, speculator investors reacted as though they had individually discovered a great secret. Their hunger drove up the prices. Savvy speculators recognized the peak approaching, realized their money had been made, and then got out. Countless others, realizing their cash was needed elsewhere and caught unaware, bailed out as the bubble burst. When the prices reached bottom, many of the cars found their way into the hands of true connoisseurs and a true value was established.

All of this sad historical rehash is by way of crystal ball gazing. There is still a lot of discussion, even argument among enthusiasts—now that the speculators and investors are out of the market—about the future of the automobile market. Will it rise again, drop further, or hold? If one accepts Robert Hoye's wisdom, look for the next roller coaster ride in 60 years after the previous one, or about 2030, with a peak arriving in 2039 or 2040. Yet Hoye's point is that, over time, the 275GTB4 has been an excellent investment for the connoisseur.

Within the exotic car world, everyone knows stories of enthusiasts who bought pontoon-fender Testarossas for $3,000 or 375 Mille

Miglias for $6,000 three decades ago and rode the rocket up in the late eighties, always referring to their cars as $3,000 or $6,000 race cars. While the TR peaked (in one widely reported sale) at nearly $12 million, historically significant versions can command nearly $5 million as this edition goes to press. This is, perhaps, a much truer value.

Before going further, it's important to emphasize that researching information about Ferraris (and their value) can be time-consuming and relatively expensive. If you can't afford the time and cost of research, you should reconsider buying a Ferrari (or any other exotic car for that matter). It is—and will be—an expensive investment. It is better by far to invest a few hundred dollars in books, magazines, and phone conversations so you can buy the right Ferrari at a right price—or decide to *not* buy one—than to discover an expensive mistake when it is too late.

Finding a Ferrari to buy can be done in a number of ways. While the rarest models, race cars and such, change hands among an elite level of collectors, racers, and enthusiasts, there are a number of sources easily accessible to a first-time buyer. Classified advertising sections in *AutoWeek*, and Ferrari-specific journals such as Gerald Roush's *Ferrari Market Letter, Hemmings Motor News, Cavalino,* and *Forza* magazines and even local editions of large-city Sunday newspapers have listings. The Ferrari Club of America and the Ferrari Owners Club also publish excellent newsletters.

Most ads in club newsletters are pretty straightforward. The seller knows he's reaching a reasonably knowledgeable potential buyer. The car may not be priced right but it is most likely to be as described. This does not always hold true, however, with newspaper or other magazine ads.

Ads saying "custom body by Farina" or "Borrani wire wheels" or "leather upholstery" or "Weber carburetors" together with an unexpectedly high price should raise eyebrows.

So far as memory serves, Ferrari has never built a body for one of his road cars. The bodies *all* have been built by Allemano, Bertone, Boano, Carrozzeria Touring, Ellena, Ghia, Ghia Aigle, Pinin Farina (changed to Pininfarina in 1961), Scaglietti, Stabilimenti Farina, or Vig-

nale, or one of the smaller coachbuilders such as Drogo, Fantuzzi, Neri & Bonacini, or Zagato.

Wheels were traditionally made by Borrani—first steel disks, then wire spoke with center-lock knock-off hubs—until the mid-sixties when Campagnolo alloy wheels appeared on GTB and GTS models (Borrani wires were options). Later models have Cromadora alloy wheels.

And original Ferrari interiors were always leather or in some cases cloth upholstery, naugahydes or vinyls.

Except for a few racing cars fitted with Solex carburetors, Ferraris always used Weber carburetors until the arrival of fuel injection. So finding an advertisement dropping the names of Borrani, Weber and Pininfarina is not a big deal so far as rarity is concerned.

Buying a car in Europe is a possibility but beware. Ferraris produced for European markets, especially in the seventies and eighties, were not equipped to meet U.S. smog and safety standards, and conversion would require very expensive modifications. Shipping and import duty into the U.S. can eat up any savings found in Europe (and undervaluing the car for Customs risks your losing the car). Of course salesmen are the same throughout the world, only Europeans have been at it for much longer than their American counterparts (against whom we have at least some legal recourse).

If the car was built prior to 1955 or was built for sale in England, Australia, New Zealand, or Japan, it could have right- or left-hand drive. A few of the early cars even had a reversed shift pattern.

A factor to be considered by any buyer of an exotic car is whether he wants an *original* car for investment purposes or a "driver" which he can enjoy even if it isn't totally original.

This decision alone will make a tremendous difference in initial cost and eventual maintenance. A substitute part that will work, but isn't original, can get your car back on the road quicker for less money, but it may reduce the value to some extent. It would be very wise to keep the original part so that you can offer the next buyer all the original pieces for the car—even if one should need a complete overhaul. The new owner may want to restore the car to original condition and will need that part.

Current labor rates in the better Ferrari shops run from $90 to $120 per hour depending on geographic location. Los Angeles and San Francisco are notoriously high. The labor rate plus the high cost of parts can cause a normal V-12 ring-and-valve job to run $7,000 to $8,000. A complete rebuild of a street V-12 can exceed $10,000 to $12,000.

It is therefore essential that a good engine be your first priority when buying a used Ferrari. Paint, upholstery, and even body work can be done by many competent craftsmen. But an engine overhaul is something to be done by an expert.

So how do you know whether or not the engine is good? You probably can't tell for certain but there are some checks you can make that will ease your mind. (Here again, a little investment in the time for a qualified Ferrari mechanic to look at your prospect can tell you—or save you—a great deal.)

Remove each breather cap (there is one on each side of the early Ferrari V-12 engine) and shake it to see if water from condensation has accumulated. Then check the dipstick for oil level, and look for that yellowish color that indicates water in the oil. At this time, also check the radiator cap to see if the water is clean, dirty or has evidence of oil.

Ask the owner to start the engine. A bit of exhaust smoke at this point is normal—a lot of smoke isn't. While the engine is idling, remove the radiator cap again. If there are bubbles it could indicate a blown head gasket.

When the engine water-temperature gauge reaches normal, the oil pressure at idle (around 950-1000 rpm if everything is right) should read between twenty-five and fifty percent of the gauge's range. If pressure is near the fifty-percent-range area, chances are good that the engine is in pretty good shape.

Early 250 GTs, with inside plugs, have separate O-ring cylinder gaskets which tend to go bad. It is advisable to insist on a compression and leak-down percent check on any used car you buy, and particularly so on Ferrari 250 GTs. The inside-plug engines also had trays around the carburetors to catch fuel overflow which could start a fire if a loose plug wire caused arcing when a carburetor flooded. Make sure these trays are installed and draining properly.

Next, ask the owner to drive the car while you observe from outside. Minor smoke from the pipes is acceptable, and fairly normal—particularly on older-model Ferraris. Heavy smoke on acceleration indicates worn valve guides; heavy smoke on deceleration means worn rings. If bad enough, either condition will call for cylinder head removal before too long.

Ferrari exhaust smoke is almost always caused by excessive wear of the valve guides and valve stems. Ferrari valve guide material is rather soft by American standards, and wear in this area will allow an excessive amount of oil to find its way into the combustion chambers and then into the exhaust system.

While observing the car from the outside, check to see if it tracks straight. If it "crab tracks," it likely means the car has been in an accident and wasn't properly repaired, or is in need of alignment in the later models with independent rear suspension.

A Ferrari V-12 engine is one of the smoothest running, and most responsive, engines ever installed in an automobile. If the idle is rough, it could be bad carburetor adjustment, or it could be worn carburetor shafts. The former isn't difficult to fix; the latter is, because it means replacement of the shafts.

Now it's time to drive the car. Because of the (probably) stiff clutch, and low inertia of the engine, it is difficult for the first-time Ferrari driver to move off smoothly. Practice will solve this problem.

A hissing noise from the clutch/transmission area might indicate worn shift forks, which is not a major problem. You can test for clutch slippage by quickly taking the car from stop up to about 6000 rpm in third gear. If the clutch is weak, the engine will suddenly over-rev for the indicated speed.

Once under way, watch the oil pressure gauge while cornering, particularly if driving vigorously. If pressure drops, chances are the oil pump pick-up hose is bad and needs replacing. Try downshifting without double-clutching. If it goes smoothly, the synchromesh rings are good. If downshifting can't be done smoothly, without a crunch, chances are pretty good that the transmission may need looking into (this is based on the assumption that the driver is somewhat competent—a ham-fisted driver won't complete a smooth, quiet shift with the best synchromesh in the world). And a Ferrari with rear-mounted transmission—275 GTB, 330 GTC, etc.—is difficult to shift from first to second when cold, even with a good transmission.

Unless you are determined, and very dedicated, try to buy a Colombo-engined Ferrari. The "big-block" Lampredi V-12s have problem areas that are hard to deal with, now that parts are almost unobtainable.

On the Lampredi engines, the cylinders are screwed into the heads, eliminating head gasket problems, but the sealing rings at the bottom of the cylinders go bad from age, or just sitting around, and leak water into the oil. Also, if the timing chain is loose, it wears a hole in a water passage at the top of the timing gear case, letting water into the oil.

You should buy a Pininfarina-bodied car if possible and, better yet, one that has lived in the southwestern part of the United States all its life. No evident rust prevention measures have been taken on some Scaglietti-bodied cars, and already rusted body panels have been seen to be installed on cars. The outside was, of course, cleaned and prepped for painting, but the inside was not de-rusted before assembly.

Okay, now that you have, or are about to get, your Ferrari, how do you take care of it so it will take care of you?

First, unless you plan to do all your own work (possible, but not necessarily recommended), you need a mechanic. He doesn't have to be a Ferrari specialist—although that is decidedly an advantage—but the key word here is *mechanic*, not a parts changer. Equipped with a full complement of metric tools, and a thorough working knowledge of carburetors, ignitions, suspension, and steering, he'll be able to work on the Ferrari.

There are tricks and peculiarities of any car, but if the person is a real mechanic, he'll learn the tricks or know where to look to get answers. If he is merely a parts changer, you shouldn't let him near your Chevy or Ford, either. One of the best mechanics Dean found for his 250 GT was a Mercedes-Benz specialist, but he was an old-timer who understood engines and their various ancillary components.

Dean owned three Ferraris, and not one of them required carburetion or ignition adjustments after they were set up (by Bill Rudd) correctly at the start. Two of the three (a 250 and a 340 Mexico) ran for three years without further adjustments.

Dean's system was: a) don't tinker with the car (other than a straightforward change of spark plugs or oil and filter), and b) warm-up the car thoroughly before driving it hard.

The engine, transmission, and driving axle assembly of any car is designed to operate best when the cases and internal moving parts are up to designated operating temperatures. This is especially critical for efficiency and longevity of cars with moving parts running in aluminum or magnesium cases.

Each morning (or after the car had not been run for several hours), after starting the engine, Dean ran it at a steady 1000 rpm for about a minute, then for maybe thirty seconds at 1500-2000 rpm. Revving a *cold* engine up and down from idle to 4000 or 5000 rpm may sound great, but does terrible things to stressed parts. You hear a lot of this at races, and the driver or mechanic doing it will tell you that he's "keeping the plugs clean." This may be true, but he's also on an ego trip. Hopefully he's already warmed the engine so that parts are up to temperature.

Following the brief engine warm-up, Dean drove the first few miles at no more than 3000 rpm or thirty to thirty-five miles per hour until he felt both transmission and drive axle were also up to running temperature. The engine temperature gauge is a pretty good indication if the car is warmed up, because all three assemblies will reach optimum at about the same time.

Once these working parts are up to design temperatures, you can drive a Ferrari about as hard as you want to. It is rugged, durable, and reliable—if you take care of it!

A Ferrari won't fail its owner unless he's done something stupid with it. A Ferrari is a relatively complex vehicle, but it is not delicate or fragile. If you take care of it, you probably won't be let down. There will be exceptions, of course, but you could find those with any make of car.

Aside from the emotional aspect of owning and driving a Ferrari, the investment potential, as investment adviser Robert Hoye knows, is probably the best you can find in a transportation device of any kind. The smallest increase in Ferrari values has been with the 12-cylinder so-called production cars: these have only slightly increased their value in the past 10 years. During the same period, any competition model has experienced a real, lasting increase in value of eight to ten times, some even more. A 1963 250 GTO that could have been purchased for $8,500 in 1971 will now bring upwards of $4 million, and other Ferraris, mainly competition models, have followed suit. A pontoon-fender 250 Testarossa, a 250 SWB California Spyder, 375MM or 250LM, for example, are selling for $2 million to $4 million and, according to Hoye, these values have begun to inch upwards sensibly.

The best news with cars returning to more sensible prices is that their insurance costs have decreased as well. It is once again possible to purchase and regularly operate an older Ferrari. Daily-use insurance premiums for older V-12s are not much different from insurance rates on current production models.

Most fortunate are the owners of the "$3,000 Testarossas" and the "$6,000 375s" who will still race them in historic and vintage events. These owners understand what the enthusiasts and connoisseurs know and the speculators never understood. Enzo Ferrari meant for his cars to be driven and raced. We can and should admire these individuals because we can to go Laguna Seca, Sears Point, Elkhart Lake, Watkins Glen, Summit Point, Road Atlanta, or any of another dozen venues where they hold these races. There we can still see—and hear—a Ferrari V-12 at full speed. It's a magnificent sight and a glorious, stirring sound.

Explanation of the star ratings on the following page:

The demise of the speculator-collector car market since the third edition of this guide was completed has changed the values of Ferraris only when measured against gold bullion, mutual funds, 401(k)s, or silver dollars stuffed in socks below the bed. This guide and others published do not normally address the relative values of the cars in comparison to other investments nor do they place them even in the context of other cars. A number of people interviewed for this book concurred on one point. Comparing Ferraris one against the other provides only half the measure of the car. The general assessment was that, in comparing Ferraris to almost any other car an enthusiast might consider, it is important to understand that the floor level—that is, a Ferrari rated at only one star—is probably two or three stars above nearly any other automobile. Except, of course, for the Ferrari rated at two, three, four, or five stars. Those are really six, seven, or eight-star cars.

Of course, one collector's starry sky is another's dark night. During this same period since the third edition was completed, one of the major domestic car manufacturers commissioned a survey among young Americans who had recently earned their driving licenses. An overwhelming majority—something like nine-to-one—expressed a preference for any AM General Hummer over any Ferrari if cost was no object.

Visibility has much to do with it. Hummers won the war in the Gulf and Hummers won over Schwartzenegger and Stallone. It has been a long time since Ferrari won a world manufacturer's championship, 1979 in fact. For many collectors, the decades before that win correspond with the times we were in school, times when we memorized magazine reviews and racing reports and established the mental wish lists that propel us to buy this guide and others.

There is absolutely no reason to despair over youthful disrespect or speculator fickleness. Ferraris, like fine wine, great caviar, excellent accommodations, and bespoke suits are emblems of tastes acquired when the wealth to allow them is acquired as well. It is easy, when the pocketbook affords fourth-hand, worn-out econoboxes, to dismiss high-performance luxury in favor of in-your-face statement-making. But nearly as inevitable as death and taxes is aging and maturation. Views change, perspectives shift, and something about Pininfarina's lines and Colombo's or Lampredi's engines become, like our parent's ideas, much more acceptable.

This fourth edition is for those of us who already know. It is also for those with something yet to learn.

Investment rating

★ ★ ★ ★ ★ The best and usually the rarest. Highest prices, highest values, and best probability of some further appreciation. These are usually sold like fine works of art, by word of mouth between knowledgeable insiders. You won't find these in newspapers or magazines and only rarely in auctions. Some prices are in seven-figures and are stable.

★ ★ ★ ★ Almost the best. Prices are in mid-six figures. Like "the best," they seldom appear in newspaper or magazine ads and if they are, they're snapped up immediately. The investment potential will be "the best" because there are usually more potential buyers (when you want to sell) in this bracket than in the five-star category.

★ ★ ★ Excellent value. These are well-regarded cars becoming subtly more so as they age. In this category you find the best combination of desirability and driveability. With all Ferrari prices more realistic than five years ago, these cars can be enjoyed. Some of the cars in this category actually can be found for less than six-figures and many represent a much higher enjoyment rating.

★ ★ A category of well-kept secrets. Generally cars came down to this rating from three-stars as a result of changes in price, not quality or desirability. In here are many of the V-12 2+2s, long undervalued and rarer now than five years ago as some individuals cut them up for parts or to rebody them as more valuable replicars.

★ Cars in this category ended up here because, as recent production models, there are still far too many of them around. They are here not because they are not good, merely they are too plentiful. Or, as "gray market" cars, they present a buyer with potential difficulty meeting current state or federal emissions standards.

The single most important factor in buying a used Ferrari is to find one with a good engine. In early 1996, you could buy a 250 GT or 330 GT 2+2 for as little as $25,000-30,000. But if the engine needed a substantial amount of work, you can end up with another $10,000-12,000 in an engine overhaul, and you'd still have only a $25,000-30,000 car.

On the following pages is a brief description of the Ferrari models most likely to be found for sale. Only "street" or "road" cars are listed in individual chapters because the probability of finding a racing car is very slight. Consequently, the rare, exotic, and competition cars are covered in a single chapter.

The years of manufacture—the model years—are as accurate as it is possible to determine. But in some cases, the production run might have begun in the early part of the year while in others, it began late in the year. Serial number parameters, where listed (say, 0429-0921) indicate that all of the model series were built within the first and last numbers of that model.

Following the model descriptions are a list of authorized U.S. and Canadian Ferrari dealers. Your own local telephone directory should be the final word. There is also a list of Ferrari owners clubs throughout the world. Finally, there is a list of recommended reading, a listing of good, accurate books in—and sadly—out of print.

Chapter 1

250 Europa GT 1954-55

Manufacture was started in late 1954 on what is generally conceded to be the first production Ferrari. It was a second-series Europa, with the 2953 cc Colombo engine and 102.3-inch wheelbase, designated Europa GT. The first of this series had serial number 0357 GT, and the last of the series was numbered 0427GT, built early in 1956.

These Ferraris were not production cars in the sense that we think of production today. But for a small, specialist car company it was a period of "arrival" as a builder of touring cars. The chassis were as nearly alike as Ferrari could make them at the time, and most bodies were by Pinin Farina— again, nearly identical, although a few cars had Vignale bodywork.

Near the end of the model run, in late 1955, Pinin Farina began developing the lower hood and flattened-oval radiator opening that was to become the standard Ferrari shape for the coming years.

The Europa GT was the first road Ferrari to use coil springs at the front. Previous models, which were long wheelbased (110 inches) with Lampredi engines, had a single, transverse-leaf front spring. All had independent front suspension, however, and be two semi-elliptic springs and a live axle at the rear, located by parallel trailing arms on each side, were continued from previous Ferrari designs.

Ferrari mechanical specifications were the most sophisticated of any car built in that period, and were the direct results of racing development. More common was the room-full-of-engineers designing and then develop-it-on-our-proving-ground approach used by the majority of the world's automobile manufactures.

These early Ferraris were fantastic automobiles when compared to their contemporaries. Powerful V-12 engine with performance to match, the most beautiful automotive sounds in the world, precise all-sychromesh transmissions, and superb handling characteristics made the Ferrari driver king of the road.

But, they are not all that pleasant to drive by today's standards. The steering is heavy, the ride is harsh, and those enormous drum brakes that look so impressive are affected by wear and improper adjustment.

They were visually attractive cars with good lines, well-fitting body panels and leather interiors, but often looked unfinished in areas such as the engine and trunk compartments.

The 250 Europa GT set the stage, and philosophy, for Ferraris to follow; exciting, handsome, charismatic, and, in reality, no better or worse than thousands of other cars. But they were fast, made beautiful noises, and had no performance equal on road or track.

Two first-series Europas with the Lampredi V-12, and 110-inch wheelbase. Subsequent Europa Gts had 102.3-inch wheelbase. *Pininfarina*

Europa GT by Vignale (serial number 0359GT), was built for Princess Liliana de Rethy. Designer Michelotti copied the wraparound windshield so popular in the mid-fifties. *Batchelor*

250 Europa GT

Engine

Type	Colombo-designed, 60-degree V-12
Bore x stroke, mm/inches:	73x58.8/2.870x2.315
Displacement, cc/cubic inches:	2953/180.0
Valve operation:	Single overhead camshaft on each bank with roller followers and rocker arms to inclined valves
Compression Ratio:	8.5:1
Carburetion:	Three Weber twin-choke, downdraft
Bhp (Mfr):	220 @ 7000

Chassis & drivetrain

Clutch:	Twin dry-plate
Transmission:	Four-speed, all-synchromesh, direct drive in fourth
Rear suspension:	Live axle with semi-elliptic springs, located by parallel trailing arms, and lever-action shock absorbers
Axle ratio:	4.85, 4.57, or 4.25:1
Front suspension:	Independent with unequal-length A-arms, coil springs, and level-action shock absorbers
Frame:	Welded tubular steel, ladder type

General

Wheelbase, mm/inches:	2600/102.3
Track, front, mm/inches:	1354/53.3
rear, mm/inches:	1349/53.1
Brakes:	Aluminum drums with iron liners
Tire size, front and rear:	6.00-16
Wheels:	Borrani wire, center-lock, knock-off
Body builder	Pinin Farina or Vignale

Interior of de Rethy coupe was unique to this car, yet similar to other Ferraris of the period. Full set of instruments is Ferrari trademark. *Batchelor*

Colombo-designed V-12 in the Europa GT had twin distributors, driven off front of camshafts, spark plugs on the inside of the heads, and single air cleaner. *Batchelor*

Number 0407GT appears to be the transition between the Europa styling and the 250 GT. The hood slopes down to a flattened-oval air intake which would become standard. *Pininfarina*

Chapter 2

Serial Nos. 0429GT-0923GT
★★★

250 GT Boano/ Ellena 1956-58

The Pinin Farina prototype 250 GT, number 0429GT, shared the Ferrari stand at the Geneva auto show in March 1956, with a Boano-built 250 GT cabriolet and a Pinin Farina 410 Superamerica. *Auto Italiana* reported in its April 20, 1956, issue that Ferrari would sumultaneously market the Pinin Farina coupe and the Boano cabriolet.

In fact, the Boano organization built, with slight changes, the Pinin Farina-designed coupe through the 1958 models, and Farina brought out its own open car in 1957. The first appearance of a Boano-built 250 GT coupe was at the Paris Salon in October 1956.

After the 1957 models, Mario Boano left his company to work in Fiat's Styling department, and Carrozzeria Boano was taken over by Luciano Pollo and Ezio Ellena. The 1958 250 GT coupes were built by a company which carried Ellena's name, but was, in fact, the same company that had built the 1956 and 1957 GT coupes. Unlike Farina, Vignale, Bertone, and Ghia, Boano and Ellena never put their names on their cars; so you won't find a bodymaker's insignia on these models.

During the years of the Pinin Farina-Boano/Ellena collaboration, the Ferrari theme developed further into its present clean, simple style. The styling had evolved from he exciting, but often bizarre, designs of Michelotti (for Vignale) into the smooth sophisticated, and often

understated, elegance associated with Farina.

The 1956 and 1957 Boano coupes had low roofs with side vent windows, and a few cars has a reversed shift pattern for the four-speed transmission. In 1958, in the Ellena-built coupes, the vent windows were eliminated, the roof was raised about two inches for increased headroom, and a standard shift pattern was adopted for all models.

Passenger comfort and luggage space were being improved with each successive body change, and the panel and trim fit of these Boano/Ellena-built cars was superb. A heater was standard, but no other extras were offered.

Another thing lacking in these early cars was adequate parking protection. The sides were almost flat, with no rub strip or body molding attached where it could do any good, and the bumpers were made of material only marginally thicker than body sheet metal. The bumpers were strictly decorative, not protective.

Body hardware items—door latches, window winding mechanisms, heater and controls, windshield wipers—were usually proprietary components from contemporary Fiats or Alfa Romeos. This kept original cost down a bit, and made parts replacement both easier and less expensive—then and now.

This Ferrari series was a pace-setter and style-setter, and yet, is currently one of the lowest-priced groups of the make.

Pinin Farina's 1956 prototype (0429GT) has break
in beltline at rear door-edge, and Farina emblem on
fender ahead of door. *Pininfarina*

Boano 1957 production model has smooth beltline,
no emblem. *Ferrari*

Early Ferrari engines such as this 250 GT V-12, had "hairpin" or "mousetrap" valve springs. This was Gioacchino Colombo's idea to reduce engine height by reducing valve stem length. Combined with small, light valves, this type of spring is very resistant to valve float at high rpms. The first Ferrari engines to use coil springs were the Testa Rossas, and all subsequent Ferrari engines used the coils. *Karl Dedolph*

250 GT Boano/Ellena

Engine
Type: . . . . .Colombo-designed, 60 degree V-12
Bore x strok, mm/inches: 73x58.8/2.870x2.315
Displacement, cc/cubic inches: 2953/180.0
Valve operation: . . . . .Single overhead camshaft on each bank with roller followers and rocker arms to inclined valves
Compression ratio: 8.5:1
Carburetion: . . . . .Three Weber twin-choke, downdraft
Bhp (Mfr): . . . . .240 @ 7000

Chassis & drivetrain
Clutch: . . . . .Twin dry-plate
Transmission: . . .Four-speed, all-synchromesh, direct drive in fourth
Rear Suspension: . . .Live axle with semi-elliptic springs, located by parrallel training arms, and lever action shock absorbers
Axle ratio: . . . .#4.57, 4.25, 3.78, or 3.67.1
Front suspension: . . . .Independent with unequal-ength A-arms, coil springs, and lever-action shock absorbers
Frame: . . . . .Welded tubular steel, ladder type

General
Wheelbase, mm/inches: 2600/102.3
Track, front, mm/inches: 1354/53.3
    rear, mm/inches: 1349/53.1
Brakes: .Aluminum drums with iron liners
Tire size, front and rear 6.00-16
Wheels: . . . . .Borrani wire, center-lock, knock-off
Body builder: . . . . .Boano or Ellena (Pinin Farina design)
*4.00:1 added in 1957

Trunk of the 1956-57 Boano coupe was not spacious, but there was more room for luggage behind the seats. Gas tank filler is inside trunk. *Monteverdi*

Interior of 1958 Boano/Ellena coupe shows Veglia instruments common to Ferraris of the period and under-dash heater as used in contemporary Alfa. *Batchelor*

High-roof 1958 250 GT (0821GT) had simple, elegant lines and excellent panel fit throughout. Bumpers are strictly decorative. Drive visibility is superb. *Batchelor*

1958 Boano/Ellena high-roof design (0821GT) has no window vents, beltline break, or emblems. *Batchelor*

Chapter 3

Serial Nos. 0503GT-1523GT
★★★★★

250 GT Berlinetta "Tour de France" 1956-59

Sports car racing had progressed so far by 1955 that the cars were virtually two-passenger Grand Prix cars. After the tragic Le Mans accident in 1955, where one driver and seventy-nine spectators died, there was a clamor to return to the classic type of racing. As a result, the Federation Internationale de l'Automobile (FIA) established new Grand Touring classes for 1956. Ferrari, with help from Pinin Farina, was ready.

Farina had built lightweight aluminum bodies on Ferrari chassis since 1952, but displayed his best design to date at the Geneva show in March 1956.

These 250 GT long-wheelbase (102.3 inches) berlinettas, slightly changed from the show car, were built by Scaglietti to Pinin Farina's design and became the customer competition car for 1956-59. The cars in this series all had odd serial numbers, making them "production" road cars, and received FIA homologation because the mechanical specifications were identical to the Boano/Ellena coupes being built at the same time. Only the bodies were different.

Weight was saved by the use of aluminum for the body, instead of steel as on the road cars; perspex side and rear windows, instead of tempered safety glass; virtually no interior hardware or trim; and the hood lifted off to give total accessibility.

The GT berlinettas started out with exposed headlights slightly recessed into the front fenders. Subsequent models had the headlights moved further into the fenders, and were covered by molded perspex which was faired into the fender shape. In 1959, a small chrome bezel surrounded a more conventional headlamp mounting.

Mechanical components of this series were almost all interchangeable with other contemporary 250 GTs, but the handmade body parts wouldn't interchange. The panels were smooth, and fit well to each other, but a door from one car wouldn't even come close to fitting the door opening in the body of another look-alike GT berlinetta.

Because the engine and chassis were the same as the production coupes, the berlinettas could be driven in town as easily as any contemporary car, and yet were tough competitors in racing. Oliver Gendebien finished third overall in the 1957 Mille Miglia, driving a 250 GT berlinetta, beating a large number of sports racing cars.

Because of its road/racing concept, there were no creature comforts offered. The lack of interior insulation would probable make a radio a worthless addition because passengers wouldn't be able to enjoy it. The enjoyment of this car comes from the pleasure of driving it.

Early in 1959, a variation of the 250 GT "Tour de France" appeared. The chassis was unchanged, but the body work (also Farina-designed, Scaglietti-built) was softer and more rounded than previous versions. In addition to the changes in contours, this interim model had roll-up windows with vent wings and quarter-windows where before there had been various louvered arrangements.

Pinin Farina displayed its berlinetta in the fall of 1955. It had louvers behind the door, tailfins, and a busy grille design. *Pininfarina*

At Geneva, in the spring of 1956, another Pinin Farina berlinetta appeared, still with louvers, high rear fenders but no fins, and different, busy grille. *Pininfarina*

---

250 GT berlinetta (LWB)
Tour de France

Engine

Type: . . . . .Colombo-designed, 60-degree V-12
Bore x stroke, mm/inches: 73x58.8/2.870x2.315
Displacement, cc/cubic inches: 2953/180.0
Valve operation: . . . . .Single overhead camshaft on each
    bank with roller followers and rocker arms to inclined valves
Compression ratio: 8.57:1
Carburetion: . . . . .Three Weber twin-choke, downdraft
Bhp (Mfr): . . . . .260 @ 7000

Chassis & drivetrain

Clutch: . . . .*Single dry-plate
Transmission: . . . .Four-speed, all sychromesh, direct drive in fourth
Rear Suspension: . . . . .Live axle with semi-elliptic springs,
    located by parallel trailing arms, and lever-action shock absorbers

Axle ratio: . . . . .4.57, 4.25, 4.00, 3.78, or 3.67:1
Front suspension: . . . . .Independent with unequal-length
    A-arms, coil springs, and lever-action shock absorbers
Frame: .Welded tubular steel, ladder type

General

Wheelbase, mm/inches: 2600/102.3
Track, front, mm/inches: 1354/53.3
    rear, mm/inches: 1349/53.1
Brakes: .Aluminum drums with iron liners
Tire size, front and rear: 6.00-16
Wheels: . . . . .Borrani wire, center-lock, knock-off
Body builder: . . . . .Scaglietti (Pinin Farina design)
*1956-57 berlinettas had twin-disc clutches; 1958-59 models had a single-disc clutch.

23

By 1957, the Scaglietti-built (to Pinin Farina design) 250 GT berlinetta was starting to look right. Extra lights were for rallies and 24-hour races. *Ferrari*

Same basic car and engine, in two configurations. The 1958 model (0925GT) has the single air cleaner and was primarily a road car; while the late

1958-59 model, right, has the cold-air box seen on competition cars. *Batchelor*

Serial number 0925GT is a 1958-model 250 GT berlinetta. This one was Bill Harrah's first Ferrari and was in Harrah's Automobile Collection in Reno until the collection was sold. It was a road car and used by him as daily transportation when new. It is fairly luxurious for this model.

Number 1353GT is a 1959 250 GT berlinetta and is fairly typical of the series. It was a competition car and has a stark interior. *Batchelor*

The 250 GT berlinetta interior is all business. Gauges include 300 kilometers per hour speedometer, 8000 rpm tach, water temperature, oil pressure, ammeter, fuel, and clock. *Batchelor*

A rare model, the 250 GT berlinetta with body by Zagato. These were lightweight cars for competition, and were successfully campaigned by private entrants in Europe. *Strother MacMinn*

The "interim" long-wheelbase berlinetta displayed the softer body lines of the ucoming 250 GT short-wheelbase model, while sharing the chassis with the older cars. *Batchelor*

Chapter 4

250 GT Cabriolet— Series I 1957-59

Even though open Ferraris had been seen since the first Ferrari in 1947, it wasn't until ten years later that convertible Ferraris were produced in series.

Farina chose the 1957 Geneva auto show in March to show a 250 GT cabriolet. This car (0655GT) later became the personal transportation for Ferrari team driver Peter Colllins. On the right side, it looked much as subsequent cabriolets would look; but on the left side, the door was cut down much in the manner of the T series MGs.

Designers of these early cabriolets seemed to be groping for a look, and they found it by the time the fourth one had been built—the design became classic.

This short series of cars is characterized by vertical front bumperettes and horizontal rear bumpers, no side vents on the fenders (although a few of the very early examples had vents similar to the 410 Superamerica) and, until the last of the series, each had headlights covered by clear perspex faired into the front fenderlines. Toward the end of this series, in 1958, the headlights moved out onto the front of the fenders, with no covering, and the front bumper became a horizontal crossbar, which was to become the norm.

The cabriolet chassis was identical to that of the Boano coupes being produced at the same time: welded oval tubular steel ladder-type frame with independent front and live rear axle, and drum brakes. The Colombo engine had the spark plugs located inside the vee, and some had a single distributor at the back of the engine.

Peter Collins's car was equipped with Dunlop disc brakes at the Dunlop headquarters in England.

Keeping track of Ferraris is a confusing task. For example, the Spyder California was in production before production stopped on the cabriolet. Both are convertibles in the American idiom, with roll-up windows, and the basic body design of the two is similar enough to look identical to the uninitiated. Remember, though, that the cabriolets were designed and built by Pinin Farina, while the Spyder California is a Pinin Farina design built by Scaglietti. Look for the bodymaker's insignia.

The cabriolet also has an all-steel body, whereas the California can be steel with aluminum doors, hood, and deck lid, or all aluminum. There will be little difference in handling or driveability, except in racing conditions where the lighter weight of the California will be an advantage.

The Spyder California is far more valuable because of its dual-purpose concept. It was actually advertised by Ferrari as a road car you can race, which the cabriolets were not.

The first Pinin Farina spyder (not to be confused with the Spyder California) was number 0655GT, built in 1957. Very little of the styling was carried over to future models. *Pininfarina*

Number 0795GT, built later in 1957, had more of the upcoming characteristics, but still had no window vents. *Karl Dedolph*

A 1958 Pinin Farina spyder in front of the Ferrari factory in Maranello. A Pinin Farina 250 GT coupe is in the background. *Factory photo by A. Villani & Figli.*

250 GT cabriolet — Series 1

Engine

Type: .Colombo-designed, 60-degree V-12

Bore x stroke, mm/inches: 73x58.8/2.870x2.315

Displacement, cc/cubic inches: 2953/180.0

Valve operation: . . . . .Single overhead camshaft on
each bank with roller followers and rocker arms to inclined valves

Compression ratio: 8.5:1

Carburetion: . . . . .Three Weber win-choke, downdraft

Bhp (Mfr): . . . . .240 @ 7000

Chassis & drivetrain

Clutch: . . . . .Twin dry-plate

Transmission: . . .Four-speed, all-synchromesh, direct drive in fourth

Rear suspension: . . . .Live axle with semi-elliptic springs, located by
parallel trailing arms, and lever-action shock absorbers

Axle ratio: . . . . .4.57, 4.25, 3.78, or 3.67:1

Front suspension: . . . .Independent with unequal-length A-arms, coi
springs, and lever-action shock absorbers

Frame: . . . . .Welded tubular steel, ladder type

General

Wheelbase, mm/inches: 2600/102.3

Track, front, mm/inches: 1354/53.3

rear, mm/inches 1349/53.1

Brakes: .Aluminum drums with iron liners

Tire size, front and rear: 6.00-16

Wheels: . . . . .Borrani wire, center-lock, knock-off

Body builder: . . . . .Pinin Farina

A *Speciale* show car for Turin in 1957 was this Pinin Farina spyder number 0709GT. *Montovani/Pininfarina*

Chapter 5

Serial Nos. 0769GT-1715GT (LWB)
★★★★★

250 GT Spyder California 1957-60

Although the first Spyder California was built in December 1957, *this* model went into production in May 1958. The chassis and engine were identical to that used in the 250 GT long-wheelbase berlinettas and, like the berlinetta, the design was by Pinin Farina and the actual construction was by Scaglietti.

Two men claim credit for the California; Johnny von Neumann, Ferrari's West Coast distributor at the time, and David Cunningham in New York City. Since mid-1957 Pinin Farina had built touring cabriolets with full interiors. Von Neumann wanted a lightened open car—like the racing berlinettas—especially for the West Coast market. The factory created the California Spyder. Cunningham's claim, however, carries a footnote that enhances its credibility. His close friend George Arnets of the North American Racing Team (NART) got No. 0769, the first one built.

It is difficult for the uninitiated to tell the California and cabriolet apart; but, basically, the cabrio has a wider grille, vertical front bumperettes (until mid-1958), faired-in headlights, wraparound windshield with side windwings, no air outlets in the front fender sides, and a rounded rear fender design with the lights at the top.

The California has a narrower, oval grille opening, side vents in the front fenders, a less-pronounced wraparound windshield, and vertical taillights at the top of the rear fenders. Other than the top, the body is very similar to the 250 GT berlinetta.

Like other 250 GTs of the period, including the berlinetta, drum brakes were still used, as were lever-action shock absorbers. In fact, all mechanical specifications were the same for the California, berlinetta, cabriolet, and coupe that were built at the same time, even with three different body builders (Pinin Farina, Boano/Ellena, and Scaglietti).

The combination of rarity (less than fifty long-wheelbase California's were built), competition capability, and appearance cause these to be some of the most sought-after Ferraris. They looked great when they were built, and they still look great today. Not everyone wants open-air driving, but for those who do, this is most desirable.

A 1958 long-wheelbase Spyder California (0923GT) has the lines that were to be characteristic of this series. *Marshall Mathews*

A 1959 LWB Spyder (1501GT) has front bumper over-riders and driving lights in grille, but otherwise is like the 1958 LWB. *Pete Coltrin*

Engine compartment of 1501GT. The "trombette" air intake stacks were sometimes factory-fitted, sometimes retrofitted. Twin Marelli distributors were standard on this model. *Pete Coltrin.*

250 GT Spyder California (LWB)

Engine

Type: . . . . .Colombo-designed, 60-degree V-12
Bore x stroke, mm/inches: 73x58.8/2.870x2.315
Displacement, cc/cubic inches: 2953/180.0
Valve operatoin: . . . . .Single overhead camshaft on each
  bank with roller followers and rocker arms to inclined valves
Compression ratio: 8.57:1
Carburetion: . . . . .Three Weber twin-choke, downdraft
Bhp (Mfr): . . . . .260 @ 7000

Chassis & drivetrain

Clutch: . . . . .Twin dry-plate
Transmission: . . .Four-speed, all-synchromesh, direct drive in fourth
Rear suspension: . . . .Live axle with semi-elliptic springs, located by
  parallel trailing arms, and lever-action shock absorbers
Axle ratio: . . . . .4.57, 4.25, 4.00, 3.78, or 3.67:1
Front suspension: . . . . . . .Independent with unequal-length A-arms,
  coil springs, and lever-action shock absorbers
Frame: . . . . .Welded tubular steel, ladder type

General

Wheelbase, mm/inches: 2600/102.3
Track, front, mm/inches: 1354/53.3
  rear, mm/inches: 1349/53.1
Brakes: . . . . .Aluminum drums with iron liners
Tire size, front and rear: 6.00-16
Wheels: . . . . .Borrani wire, center-lock, knock-off
Body builder: . . . . .Scaglietti (Pinin Farina design)

Minor differences can be seen in the interiors of 9923GT above, and 1501GT such as door trim and placement of window crank. *Marshall Mathews*

Clean, classic lines of the LWB Spyder California, built by Scaglietti to Pinin Farina design. *Jay L. Traub*

Chapter 6

250 GT PF Coupe 1958-62

A new Pinin Farina-bodied 250 GT coupe was shown at the Paris Salon in October 1958. It was a 1959 model, and would replace the Boano/Ellena coupe as the standard production Ferrari road car through 1961.

The first cars in this series shared most mechanical components with the 1958 cars—drum brakes, lever-action Houdaille shock absorbers, four-speed transmission, and spark plugs located inside the vee of the engine. One initial difference was that twin Marelli distributors replaced the single distributor used previously. This was welcome as the single unit had a habit of arcing across the contacts inside the distributor cap because the contacts were too close together. This model also had the first fresh-air heater used on a Ferrari.

The Pinin Farina body remained unchanged during the model run; but in 1960, mechanical changes were made which vastly improved the car. Spark plugs were moved to the outside of the heads and siamesed intake ports were abandoned in favor of individual ports; disc brakes replaced the sometimes dodgy drum brakes; tubular shocks were made standard equipment; overdrive was added to the four-speed transmission; and a single-disc clutch replaced the twin-disc unit previously used.

A large, set in tubular frame connected the independent front suspension with its unequal-length A-arms and coil springs, to the live rear axle which had semi-elliptic springs and was located by Ferrari's twin parallel trailing arms.

Styling of the new 250 GT was not as exciting as some other Farina designs, before or since; but it was clean, elegant, and has worn well for the last thirty years. The coupe body is almost identical to the cabriolet—the main difference being the raised rear fenders of the open cars.

Passenger space and comfort were the best of any Ferrari (other than the Superamericas) up to this point, as was luggage accommodation. These features, along with better brakes, make PF coupes some of the best touring cars of the era.

Dean Batchelor's experience of maintaining a 250 GT (actually a 1958 Ellena coupe which had the same mechanical specifications as the first PF coupes) eventually taught him to change a set of spark plugs in forty-five minutes. His first plug change took ninety minutes—because of inexperience and fear of cross-threading the plugs in their seemingly inaccessible location.

The brakes were not good by today's standards. Dean developed a practice of gently riding the pedal for the first mile in the morning because, when cold, the 14-inch drums wouldn't stop the car in a straight line. Once they warmed-up, however, they did a pretty fair job.

If this model is within your range of interest and income, a later 250 PF will be a better choice.

The first pre-production prototype set the style for the series, which continued for three years with about 350 being built. *Pininfarina*

The second pre-production prototype was shown in June 1958. By now, the design was set. *Pininfarina*

This special-bodied 250 GT (0853GT) was built in 1958 for Prince Bertil of Sweden. *Pininfarina*

Standard engine compartment of the Ferrari V-12; three Weber downdrafts covered by a single air cleaner. This was the first Ferrari with fresh-air ventilation and heater, with the air intake at the base of the windshield. *Road & Track*

250 GT PF coupe

Engine

Type: .Colombo-designed, 60-degree V-12
Bore x stroke, mm/inches: 73x58.8/2.870x2.315
Displacement, cc/cubic inches: 2953/180.0
Valve operation: . . . . .Single overhead camshaft on each
  bank with roller followers and rocker arms to inclined valves
Compression ratio: 8.57:1
Carburetion: . . . . .Three Weber twin-choke, downdraft
Bhp (Mfr): . . . . .240 @ 7000

Chassis & drivetrain

Clutch: . . . .*Single dry-plate
Transmission: . . . .*Four-speed, all-synchromesh, direct
  drive in fourth
Rear suspension: . . .*Live axle with semi-elliptic springs, located by
  parallel trailing arms, and telescopic shock absorbers
Axle ratio: . . . . .4.57, 4.25, 4.00, 3.78, or 3.67:1
Front suspension: . . . . . .*Independent with unequal-length A-arms,
  coil springs, and telescopic shock absorbers
Frame: . . . . .Welded tubular steel, ladder type

General

Wheelbase, mm/inches: 2600/102.3
Track, front, mm/inches: 1354/53.3
  rear, mm/inches: 1349/53.1
Brakes: . . . .*Disc
Tire size, front and rear: *6.00-16
Wheels: . . . . .Borrani wire, center-lock, knock-off
Body builder: . . . .*Pinin Farina
*1960-61 cars had overdrive, 1958-59 models had lever-action shock absorbers, drum brakes, and a twin-disc clutch. Tire sizes were at times 185-400, 185-15, or 6.00-16. Pinin Farina became Pininfarina in 1961

A special car was built in 1958 for an old customer. The body is standard 250 GT, but the bumpers were vertical rather than horizontal, the lower body panels were chrome and the interior had true bucket seats. *Pininfarina*

Early 1960 Pinin Farina coupe. The interior was becoming even more luxurious in the Grand Touring tradition. Seatbacks were adjustable for rake. *Road & Track*

Chapter 7

250 GT Berlinetta 1959-62

Serial Nos. 1461GT-4065GT
★ ★ ★ ★ ★
SEFAC "Hot Rods"
★ ★ ★ ★-1/2
Alloy body, racing
★ ★ ★ ★
Steel body, street

In October 1959, at the Paris Salon, a shortened version (commonly referred to as the SWB—short wheelbase) of the interim car was displayed. Front and rear shapes were almost identical to the interim berlinettas, but the 94.5-inch wheelbase necessitated elimination of the half ★ improvement in looks.

Most SWB bodies were steel with aluminum doors, hood, and trunk lid; but some all-aluminum bodies were built for the serious competitor during the three-year model run.

The Colombo-designed engine was still used, and all examples had twelve intake ports with the plugs on the outside of the heads, coil valve springs replaced the "hairpin" or "mousetrap" springs previously used, and there were four studs around each cylinder instead of three—greatly improving compression sealing. Disc brakes and tubular Koni shock absorbers also became standard.

As a result of the increased horsepower, shorter and lighter chassis, and better brakes, the SWB 250 GT was faster and handled better than its predecessors, making it formidable competition in any type of event.

These competition-oriented GT berlinettas, which carried odd serial numbers representative of the road cars, were raced and rallied with great success. The Tour de France, which was a week-long rally around France,

with eight timed events (six races and two hill-climbs) interspersed into the rally, was won by Ferrari so many times that the long-wheelbase 250 GT was called the Tour de France model. The SWB continued the winning ways.

Ferraris won the Tour de France in 1951 and from 1956 to 1961. The last two years, private customers had a more potent SWB known as the SEFAC "hot rod" with super-lightened frames and three dual-Weber 46 millimeter carburetors feeding the engine. More than 280 horsepower peaked ferociously at 5500 rpm, making the 2,400-pound car's handling on wet circuits a handful. Officially called the 168 Comp./61, probably only twenty-four were produced in 1961 and 1962.

All 250 GT berlinettas—with long or short wheelbase—are desirable collector cars because of their handsome lines and excellent performance. Because of their favored status with competitors in their day, both left- and right-hand-driver versions were produced. Steel-body street cars with 240 horsepower were docile enough to drive in traffic while the alloy body racers, with 260–275 horsepower are fast enough to join the winner's circle after a vintage race. The SEFAC "hot rods," were, of course, the rarest, but all the versions have appreciated steadily over the past decade and there's no reason to believe this will change.

Certain examples of the racing 250 GT SWB were built with large fuel tanks, placing the spare tire directly under the rear window. Racing engines were rated at 260–275 horsepower, more than 20 horsepower over the street versions. The 168 comp./61 customer racers included lightened frames and three Weber 46 millimeter dual throat carbs and produced more than 280 horsepower. Shown here is a 1960 steel "Lusso" (luxury) berlinetta, number 1993GT. *Stan Nowak*

The man himself. Enzo Ferrari at the wheel of 250 GT berlinetta. *Pete Coltrin*

Interior of the 250 SWB (3337GT) left no provision for adding creature amenities, so this owner mounted a radio on top of the transmission tunnel. The shift knob is not original. *Batchelor*

250 GT berlinetta (SWB) 168 comp./61

Engine

Type: . . . . .Colombo-designed, 60-degree V-12
Bore x stroke, mm/inches: 73x58.8/2.870x2.315
Displacement, cc/cubic inches: 2953/180.0
Valve operation: . . . . .Single overhead camshaft on each
bank with roller followers and rocker arms to inclined valves
Compression ratio: 9.2:1
Carburetion: . . . . .Three Weber twin-choke, downdraft
Bhp (Mfr): . . . . .280 @ 7000

Chassis & drivetrain

Clutch: . . . . .Single dry-plate
Transmission: . . . . .Four-speed, all-synchromesh,
direct drive in fourth
Rear suspension: . . . . .Live axle with semi-elliptic springs,
located by parallel trailing arms, and telescopic shock absorbers
Axle ratio: . . . . .4.57, 4.25, 4.00, 3.78, 3.67, 3.55, or 3.44:1
Front suspension: . . . . . . .Independent with unequal-length A-arms,
coil springs, and telescopic shock absorbers
Frame: . . . . .Welded tubular steel, ladder type

General

Wheelbase, mm/inches: 2400/94.5
Track, front, mm/inches: 1354/53.3
rear, mm/inches: 1349/53.1
Brakes: . . . . .Disc
Tire size, front and rear: *6.00-16
Wheels: . . . . .Borrani wire, center-lock, knock-off
Body builder: . . . . .Scaglietti (Pinin Farina design)
*Pre-1960 cars. 1960 and later had 175-400 or 185-15 tires.

Front and rear (3337GT) show clean shapes with general lack of ornamentation. Body is by Scaglietti to a Pininfarina design. *Batchelor*

The bodies on the 1960 and 1961 SWB berlinettas were the same, in shape and general detailing; but the 1961 had opening vent wings, and the 1960 (1993GT) did not. *Pininfarina*

One of the best all-around cars of the period, the 250 GT short-wheelbase berlinetta was at home on either road or track. Bodies were made of steel with aluminum doors, hood and trunk lid; although the serious competitor could have an all-aluminum body. *Jay L. Traub*

Chapter 8

Serial Nos. 1537GT-3803GT
★★★1/2

250 GT Cabriolet—
Series II 1959-62

Realizing the confusion that could exist between the cabriolet and Spyder, Pinin Farina took steps to separate the look of the two cars. This was fairly simple, as the California had been derived from the long-wheelbase berlinetta (both mechanically and visually); and the cabriolet was closely identified with the coupes, so the styling of the cabriolet became more like the 1959 Pinin Farina coupe.

Most Ferrari enthusiasts think the Spyders are better looking than the cabriolets, and the Spyder *does* have slightly better performance, so it is the more popular of the two designs. The Pinin Farina version, however, was conceived as a semi-luxury touring car and had better interior appointments, more soundproofing, and was better suited to the average Ferrari customer for everyday use.

The cabriolet is an elegant and understated design which, if you like it at all, wears well and withstands the test of time.

Like other Ferraris, running changes were made at various times, including the switch to disc brakes; telescopic shock absorbers replaced the Houdaille lever-action units; overdrive was added to the four-speed trans-

mission; and twin distributors replaced the single unit used initially.

The cabriolets, both Series I and II, are relatively good buys if one has to have a Ferrari. They look good, will do almost anything the other models will do (and do it as well), and the investment is lower, because other models are more popular and have appreciated faster.

Given a choice between an early and a late version of the same model (and barring some extraordinary bargain price on one or the other), always opt for the later car. It will have running mechanical changes that invariably make it a better car. The 250 cabriolet is a case in point; adoption of disc brakes, tubular shock absorbers, twin distributors, and overdrive all make the car more pleasant to drive than earlier models. Visually, you'd be hard put to tell them apart without opening the hood or looking underneath the car.

Also, when Ferrari moved the spark plugs from inside the vee to the outside of the heads, it allowed the redesign of the cylinder head which resulted in better breathing. These later engines are not only more reliable, but are easier to service if something does go wrong.

Pinin Farina cabriolet 250 GT shown with optional, removable hardtop. Classic lines were and are typical of Farina's restrained design approach. *Pininfarina*

A Pinin Farina 250 GT cabriolet inside the massive
Farina factory in Torino, Italy. *Pininfarina*

A rare Series II Pinin Farina cabriolet with the flat
hood (without air-scoop) as used on the 250 GT
coupes. *Pininfarina*

This unique 1960 SWB alloy competition "spyder speciale," serial number 1737GT, resembled several 400 Superamericas (see Chapter 21). *Pininfarina*

---

250 GT cabriolet — Series II

Engine

Type: . . . . .Colombo-designed, 60-degree V-12

Bore x stroke, mm/inches: 73x58.8/2.870x2.315

Displacement, cc/cubic inches: 2953/180.0

Valve operation: . . . . .Single overhead camshaft on each bank with roller followers and rocker arms to inclined valves

Compression ratio: 8.57:1

Carburetion: . . . . .Three Weber twin-choke, downdraft

Bhp (Mfr): . . . . .260 @ 7000

Chassis & drivetrain

Clutch: . . . .
Single dry-plate

Transmission: .Four-speed, all-synchromesh, direct drive in fourth with electrically operated overdrive (28.2%) fifth

Rear suspension: . . . . .Live axle with semi-elliptic springs, located by parallel trailing arms, and telescopic shock absorbers

Axle ratio: . . . . .4.57, 4.25, 4.00, 3.78, or 3.67:1

Front suspension: . . . . .Independent with unequal-length A-arms, coil springs, and telescopic shock absorbers

Frame: . . . . .Welded tubular steel, ladder type

General

Wheelbase, mm/inches: 2600/102.3

Track, front, mm/inches: 1354/53.3

rear, mm/inches: 1349/53.1

Brakes: . . . . .Disc

Tire size, front and rear: *6.00-16

Wheels: .Borrani wire, center-lock, knock-off

Body builder: .Scaglietti (Pinin Farina design)

*Later models had 185-15 tires.

Chapter 9

Serial Nos. 1795GT-4137GT (SWB)
★★★★★

250 GT Spyder California 1960-63

Production of the short-wheelbase Spyder Californias spanned the period from May 1960 to February 1963. During that two-and-a-half-year period only about fifty of the model were built.

Like its predecessor, the long-wheelbase California, chassis specifications were almost identical to the berlinetta that paralleled it in production: the short-wheelbase (94.5 inches) berlinetta which had gone into production in 1959.

Unlike the long-wheelbase cars, however, the body shape of the SWB California was mor like the long-wheelbase California—shortened to fit the eight-inch-shorter wheelbase—and bore no resemblance to the SWB berlinetta whose chassis it shared. The SWB California body design was a continuation of the LWB Pinin Farina shape, and built by Scaglietti in Modena.

The short-wheelbase California had more in common with its predecessor than looks and general mechanical specifications, however, as it had even better competition capabilities because of its lighter weight and better handling qualities.

The engine was the outside plug 250 V-12, and tubular shocks and disc brakes were standard. The SWB would go, turn, and stop; and it looked great! It was, in fact, advertised as a car that could be driven in normal daily use or raced. Not too many owners chose to race the Spyder Californias, as they were purchased by customers who wanted the "rub-off" from the implied association with a model built as a semi-competition car. The fact that they *didn't* race it was less important than the fact that they *could* race it if they wanted to. Most owners rightly thought that the California was just too pretty to put on a track where it would get damaged from gravel thrown by a competitor's tires or, worse, get bumped.

As good as they were, and are, the ride and handling is vintage 1960s, and by today's more demanding standards, they don't measure up. The Californias are easy-to-drive cars and quite comfortable in most driving conditions, but don't expect one to handle like a later V-12 with independent suspension, or like a 308 mid-engined V-8.

Vintage or not, the short-wheelbase Californias are some of the most sought-after Ferraris. Because of their performance and appearance, combined with scarcity, prices skyrocketed in the late 1980s.

The classic beauty of the SWB can be seen in these
photos of George Carrick's car taken by Clive Clark.

A 1961 short-wheelbase Spyder California (3077GT) is one of the prettiest of Ferraris, and it looks as good today as it did when new. *Vittorio L. Roveda*

Things to watch for: This SWB Spyder has wrong steering wheel; rearview mirror has been moved from top of dash to windshield; outside fender mirrors are aftermarket accessory mirrors: Ferrari name should not appear above emblem in front of hood; and wheels are wrong. None of this makes any difference in driveability, but disqualifies it as an original car. *Batchelor*

---

250 GT Spyder California (SWB)

Engine
Type: . . . . .Colombo-designed, 60-degree V-12
Bore x stroke, mm/inches: 73x58.8/2.870x2.315
Displacement, cc/cubic inches: .2953/180.0
Valve operation: Single overhead camshaft on each bank with roller followers and rocker arms to inclined valves
Compression ratio: 9.2:1
Carburetion: . . . . .Three Weber twin-choke, downdraft
Bhp (Mfr): . . . . .280 @ 7000

Chassis & drivetrain
Clutch: . . . .
Single dry-plate
Transmission: . . .Four-speed, all-synchromesh, direct drive in fourth
Rear suspension: . . . .Live axle with semi-elliptic springs, located by parallel trailing arms, and telescopic shock absorbers
Axle ratio: . . . . .4.57, 4.25, 4.00, 3.78, 3.67, 3.55 or 3.44:1
Front suspension: . . .Independent with unequal-length A-arms, coil springs and telescopic shock absorbers
Frame: . . . . .Welded tubular steel, ladder type

General
Wheelbase, mm/inches: 2400/94.5
Track, front, mm/inches: 1354/53.3
rear, mm/inches: 1349/53.1
Brakes: . . . . .Disc
Tire size, front and rear: *6.00-16
Wheels: . . . . .Borrani wire, center-lock, knock-off
Body builder: . . . . .Scaglietti (Pinin Farina design)
*Pre-1960 cars. 1960 and later had 175-400 or 185-15 tires.

Some short-wheelbase Spyder Californias didn't have covered headlights or side vents in front fenders. This one is missing its front bumper as well. *Batchelor*

Chapter 10

250 GT Berlinetta
Lusso 1962-64
Serial Nos. 4103GT-5955GT
★★★ 1/2 Stars

250 GT Berlinetta Lusso 1962-64

Paris, October 1962. At the annual auto show, Ferrari and Pininfarina once again introduced a new car, the 250 GT/L, which became known as the Lusso, for luxury.

Combining design elements from the competition-oriented short-wheelbase berlinettas and the 250 GTO, it was, and is, one of the handsomest Ferraris. No, make that one of the handsomest cars ever built. During its two-year life span, approximately 350 Lussos were built.

The Lusso chassis was, again, a fairly standard Ferrari design, with unequal-length A-arms and coil spring front suspension. The rear suspension was the tried-and-true semi-elliptic springs with axle location by parallel trailing arms on each side. However, two new features for a Ferrari road car were seen at the back: the telescopic shock absorbers had concentric "helper" springs wound around them, and the axle's lateral location was by Watt linkage. Both features were borrowed from the GTO. Disc brakes were also standard.

Lusso bodies were built by Scaglietti to Pininfarina's design and were of steel, with aluminum doors, hood, and trunk lid. Like too many other Ferraris, the beautiful bodywork is almost unprotected from potential parking damage. The bumpers are, at best, decorative.

The seats are genuine bucket type (unlike most previous Ferrari road cars), comparable to those found in the GT berlinettas. The seats are adjustable fore and aft, but have no back rake adjustment and don't tilt forward - so loading luggage into the area behind the seats requires physical strength and dexterity.

The instrument panel is unique to the Lusso, with a large speedometer and tachometer in the center of the panel—angled toward the driver—and the five smaller gauges mounted right in front of the driver. Vision is superb, with lots of glass area and minimal interference from windshield posts or quarter panels.

Several owners have complained about excessive noise in the cockpit due to the paucity of insulation and the low rear axle gearing (high ratio) which causes the engine to run at higher rpm than should be needed for easy cruising. On the other hand, some owners also complain of an excessively high first gear, making the Lusso a little difficult to start smoothly from a stop.

Road & Track editors conducted a road test of a five-year-old Lusso in the June 1969 issue and reported that "the wood-rimmed steering wheel is rather high, nearly vertical and isn't adjustable in any way" and although the seatbacks weren't adjustable "the brake and clutch pedals have a simple adjustment that allows moving the pads fore and aft about two inches.

During the performance tests, which netted a standing-start quarter-mile time of 16.1 seconds (91 miles per hour at the end of the quarter), they discovered the marginal clutch had started to slip after several consecutive fast starts. And, "The speedometer is as optimistic as in most Ferraris." It is widely reported that Ferrari (also Maserati and Lamborghini) speedometers run anywhere from five to fifteen percent optimistic.

These factors should not deter you from investing in a Lusso. It is still one of the more desirable of Ferraris.

The 1962-64 250 GT berlinetta Lusso was, and is, one of the handsomest Ferraris. Its classic lines, plus its rarity make it one of the most desirable of Ferraris. *Pininfarina*

The Lusso interior is unique among Ferraris, with the speedometer and tach in the center of the panel and the smaller instruments in front of the driver. *Ed Niles*

Lusso passengers learned to travel light. With spare tire and tool kit in trunk, there was little room for anything else. Some luggage can be accommodated behind the seats. *Road & Track*

---

250 GT berlinetta Lusso

Engine
Type: .Colombo-designed, 60-degree V-12
Bore x stroke, mm/inches: 73x58.8/2.870x2.315
Displacement, cc/cubic inches: 2953/180.0
Valve operation: . . . . .Single overhead camshaft on each
   bank with roller followers and rocker arms to inclined valves
Compression ratio: 9.3:1
Carburetion: . . . . .Three Weber twin-choke, downdraft
Bhp (Mfr): . . . . .250 @ 7000
Chassis & drivetrain
Clutch: . . . . .Single dry-plate
Transmission: . . . . .Four-speed, all-synchromesh,
   direst drive in fourth
Rear suspension: . . . . .Live axle with semi-elliptic springs,
   located by parallel trailing arms, and telescopic shock absorbers
Axle ratio: . . . . .4.00 or 3.78:1
Front suspension: . . . . . . .Independent with unequal length A-arms,
   coil springs, and telescopic shock absorbers
Frame: . . . . .Welded tubular steel, ladder type
General
Wheelbase, mm/inches: 2400/94/5
Track, front, mm/inches: 1395/55.0
   rear, mm/inches: 1387/54.6
Brakes: . . . . .Disc
Tire size, front and rear: 185SP-15
Wheels: . . . . .Borrani wire, center-lock, knock-off
Body builder: . . . . .Scatlietti (Pininfarina design)

Lusso engine compartment. Two distributors at the back, two breathers and two oil filters at the front. *Vintage Car Store*

In 1963, a special Lusso (4335GT) was built for Giovanni Battista Giusseppe "Pinin" Farina (he legally changed his name to Pininfarina in 1961). The car had a hood bulge, a slight spoiler on the rear, and used 400 SA-type door handles as well as no vent window on the driver's side (the Paris show car had none at all). The tach and speedo, in the center on production cars, were in front of the driver on this version. *Pininfarina*

Chapter 11

275 GTB and
GTB/C 1964-66
★★★ 1/2 275 GTB
★★★★ 1/2 275 GTB/C

275 GTB and GTB/C 1964-66

Two new Ferraris made their debuts at the 1964 Paris Salon: the 275 GTB and GTS. The chassis were identical, with the now-typicalwelded steel tubular frame, full independent suspension with unequal-length A-arms front and rear, disc brakes, and tubular shock absorbers. The engines were also identical 3.3-liter V-12s of Colombo origin, but the berlinetta engine produced 280 horsepower while the spyder engine was rated at 260.

Both models had a five-speed transmission mounted in unit with the rear axle. The clutch and bell housing were at the engine. With the rear-mounted gearbox came independent rear suspension, making the 275 GTBs the first street Ferrari to be so equipped.

The bodywork was completely different on the two cars; the spyder evolved from the 300 GT 2 + 2 (Pininfarina designed and built), but the berlinetta body was a completely new shape - a replacement for the Lusso with softer, more rounded curves, designed by the Pininfarina but built by Scaglietti.

The 275 GTB was intended for either touring or racing, and the customer had the option of either three Weber carburetors (with which the GTB was homologated for competition by the FIA) or six. The body could be steel and aluminum or all-aluminum. Campagnolo alloy wheels were standard, but the Borrani wire wheels were an option.

The body shape remained almost unchanged throughout the model run, but minor changes appeared when the first Series II cars were shown at Frankfurt in 1965. The headlight covers no longer had chrome rims, the vent wing was missing from the driver's window, and a bulge appeared on the hood to cover the carburetors. At the rear, the trunk lid hinges were on the outside of the body to allow more interior space. At the Paris show a month later, the front of the body had been lengthened and had a smaller air intake.

By the time the Series II 275 GTB was shown at the Brussels show in January 1966, the car had new alloy wheels and the drive shaft was encased in a torque tube. Approximately 250 Series I and about 200 Series II 275 GTBs were built.

In the spring of 1966, a special version, the 275 GTB/C, was built in very limited numbers (about a dozen) with serial numbers between 9007 and 9085. These 275s had special camshafts, valves, pistons, crankshaft, and carburetors, and a dry-sump lubrication system. The bodies were alumium and the cars were created expressly for competition.

The 275 series marked the progressive change in Ferrari design philosophy from thinly disguised racers to comfortable and luxurious transportation vehicles. Because of the chassis changes—primarily the four-wheel independent suspension—the 275s were not only faster, but more comfortable than their predecessors. The 275 series offered an extremely high-speed touring car (remember they were designed when there were no speed limits in most of Europe and the United States hadn't gone to 55 mile per hour yet) which gave the driver and passenger the utmost feeling of confidence. You could drive all day as fast as you cared to and arrive at your destination without the fatigue normally associated with this sort of endeavor.

The one drawback of the 275 was the somewhat notchy shift mechanism of the rear-mounted transmission. Earlier Ferraris with the transmission mounted at the back of the engine were much easier to shift. The trade-off, however, is on the side of the 275.

The 275GTB/C competition version was built in limited numbers. The engine was dry-sumped, sheet metal was thin alloy, and many chassis parts were lighter than normal. The special, curved air intake stacks—a unique feature to these cars—can be seen with the air cleaner cover removed. *Batchelor*

The 275 GTB as it was introduced in 1964. This was the first Ferrari GT to have cast-alloy wheels. *Pininfarina*

The 275 GTB introduced in Paris in October 1964, was intended to be a replacement for the Lusso. It was the first Ferrari road car to have all-independent suspension, and the transmission was in unit with the rear axle. *Warren Fitzgerald*

Interior of the 275 GTB is luxurious, and seats have fore and aft adjustment, but seatback angle is fixed. *Ed Niles*

275 GTB and GTB/C

Engine

Type: .Colombo-designed, 60-degree V-12
Bore x stroke, mm/inches: 77x58.8/3.050x2.315
Displacement, cc/cubic inches: 3286/200.5
Valve operation: . . . . .Single overhead camshaft on each
    bank with roller followers and rocker arms to inclined valves
Compression ratio: 9.2:1
Carburetion: . . . .*Three Weber twin-choke, downdraft
Bhp (Mfr): . . . . .280 @ 7600

Chassis & drivetrain

Clutch: . . . . .Single dry-plate
Transmission: . . . . .Five-speed, all-synchromesh, in unit
    with the differential, all indirect gears
Rear suspension: . . . . . . .Independent with unequal-length A-arms,
    coil springs, and telescopic shock absorbers
Axle ratio: 3.55:1
Front suspension: . . . . . . .Independent with unequal-length A-arms,
    coil springs, and telescopic shock absorbers
Frame: . . . . .Welded tubular steel, ladder type

General

Wheelbase, mm/inches: .2400/94.5
Track, front, mm/inches: .1377/54.2
rear, mm/inches: 1383/54.8
Brakes: . . . . .Disc
Tire size, front and rear: . . . . .Pirelli 210/14 HS or Dunlop
    205 HR/14SP
Wheels: . . . . .Campagnolo alloy
Body builder: . . . . .Scaglietti (Pininfarina design)
*The 275 GTB was homologated with three carburetors, but six
Webers were optional. Standard bodies were steel and aluminum,
but all-aluminum bodies were optional, as were Borrani wire wheels.

At the Frankfurt show in October 1965, this 275 appeared with slight body revisions; the rear deck hinges were outside, the driver's door had no vent window, a hood bulge was added over the carburetors and the nose was slightly longer with a smaller air intake. *Pininfarina*

A very few, very special 275 GTBs were seen in this configuration. Note the high rear fenders with louvers behind rear wheel opening. *Kurt Miska*

Chapter 12

275 GTS 1964-66

The 275 GTB (berlinetta) and GTS (spyder) were introduced simultaneously at the Paris show in October 1964. They shared identical chassis and engines, but had completely different bodies.

The 3.3 - liter engine was a continuation of the Colombo unit so familiar in Ferraris but, for the first time on a Ferrari road car (and like the 275 GTB), the transmission (a five-speed) was mounted in unit with the rear axle. The clutch was still at the back of the engine, and the drive shaft was supported by a central steady-bearing.

Suspension was independent all around, with concentric coil spring/shock absorbersand unequal-length A-ams. Disc brakes were standard on all four wheels. These were the most sophisticated Ferrari road cars to this date, as Ferrari kept updating and improving his Grand Touring vehicles.

The berlinettas were built by Scaglietti to a Pininfarina design, but the spyders (convertibles to Americans) were all Pininfarina, design and construction. The spyder front was somewhat reminiscent of the earlier 250 GT cabriolets, but the back took the shape of the 330 2+2, modified to suit the new, open body.

The GTS is beautifully finished and well-detailed, but not all drivers fit the seat/pedals/steering wheel proportions of a Ferrari. The seats are adjustable, with plenty of fore and aft movement, but not enough back rake angle adjustment. Consequently, when the seat is back far enough for a tall driver to be comfortable with the seat-to-pedal distance, the steering is likely to be too far away, and it isn't adjustable.

As a result of moving the transmission to the rear, the GTS has even better balance than most previous Ferraris, and this is apparent in driving ease and handling. In spite of the possible uncomfortable driving position, fast touring over any type road is safe and enjoyable. It is a neutral-handling car with good road adhesion.

Typical of convertibles, it is noisier than a closed car because you're getting wind and exhaust noise along with engine and drive-train sounds. The decibel level would be unacceptable to engineers of most car companies, because it wouldn't be acceptable to their customers; but in a Ferrari it doesn't seem to make that much difference, somehow.

In a 1966 road test of the 275 GTS by *Road & Track*, the standing-start quarter mile was covered in 15.7 seconds (top speed, 91 miles per hour) so it was really no faster than the Lusso. But, on a trip through Nevada the engineering editor covered 425 miles in five hours including "one gas and two lemonade stops" without fatigue or stress on either car or driver. The ambient air temperature was one hundred degrees Fahrenheit and neither the car's oil nor water temperature gauges read higher than normal at any time.

The writer commented about the noise level of the convertible top but felt it wasn't particularly offensive, and was extremel complimentary about the car's behavior on the road. This is the 275 GTB's true element, and he was using the car the way it was designed to be used. Excellent suspension and superb brakes allow extremely fast driving with comfort, confidence, and safety. And *style.*

This is a typical 275 GTS engine bay. Three down-draft Weber carburetors under a single air cleaner nestled between black crackle-finished valve covers. *Scott Malcolm/Road & Track*

The 275 GTS was introduced at the Paris Salon in October 1964. The body is by Pininfarina, but no crest is shown. *Pininfarina*

A (removable) hardtop on the 1965 275 GTS. *Pininfarina*

In 1965, changes were made to the side vents. Parking lights and front bumper over-riders were also added. A removable hardtop was offered but few were made. This is a rare accessory. *Pininfarina*

275 GTS

Engine

Type: .Colombo-designed, 60-degree V-12
Bore x stroke, mm/inches: 77x58.8/3.050x2.315
Displacement, cc/cubic inches: 3286/200.5
Valve operation: . . . . .Single overhead camshaft on each
 bank with roller followers and rocker arms to inclined valves
Compression ratio: 9.2:1
Carburetion: . . . . .Three Weber twin-choke, downdraft
Bhp (Mfr): . . . . .260 @ 7000

Chassis & drivetrain

Clutch: . . . . .Single dry-plate
Transmission: . . . . .Five-speed, all-synchromesh,
 in unit with the differential, all indirect gears
Rear suspension: . . . . . . .Independent with unequal-length A-arms,
 coil springs, and telescopic shock absorbers

Axle ratio: . . . . .3.30 or 3.55:1
Front suspension: . . . . . .Independent with unequal-length A-arms,
 coil springs, and telescopic shock absorbers
Frame: . . . . .Welded tubular steel, ladder type

General

Wheelbase, mm/inches: 2400/94.5
Track, front, mm/inches: 1377/54.2
 rear, mm/inches: 1393/54.8
Brakes: . . . . .Disc
Tire size, front and rear: . . . . .Pirelli 210/14 HS or
 Dunlop 205 HR/14SP
Wheels: . . . . .Borrani wire, center-lock, knock-off
Body builder: . . . . .Pininfarina

Chapter 13

330 GTC and GTS 1966-70

330 GTC and GTS
1966-70
Serial Nos 8329GT-11613GT
★★★ GTC
★★★★ GTS
★★★ 1/2 365 GTC
★★★★ 365 GTS

Introduced at the Geneva auto show in March 1966, the 330 GTC utilized the chasis of the 275 GTB, the engine of the 330 GT 2+2, and was covered by a Pininfarina body that took the front of the 400 Superamerica and the rear of the 275 GTS. A combination with that many variables could have been a disaster, but the entire car, mechanically and visually, works extremely well.

Even though the basic engine is like that used in the 330 2+2, the cylinder block was redesigned because, unlike the 2+2, the GTC has a rear-mounted transmission which necessitated different mountings for both engine and differential. The drive shaft goes through a torque tube to the transaxle.

Suspension is independent all around, with unequal-length A-arms, coil springs, and telescopic shock absorbers; and there are disc brakes on all four wheels.

By this time in Ferrari history, the competition and road models were completely separated, and the new GTC made no pretext of being something it wasn't. What it was, and is, is a super deluxe Grand Touring car which is fast, comfortable, and quiet. A good radio could be enjoyed, and air conditioning was an option.

Production of the 330 GTC lasted from mid-1966 to the end of 1968, at which time the engine was enlarged to 4.4 liters, and the car became a 365 GTC. This version was produced through 1969. Visually the two cars were identical except for placement of the

engine hot-air outlets which moved from the fender sides to the rear of the hood.

At the Paris Salon in October 1966, a convertible version called the 330 GTS was shown to complement the coupe. Production of the GTS continued alongside the coupe until the end of 1968; at which time it, also, became a 365 GTS, continuing through 1969.

Probably 150 365 GTC and 20 GTS cars were built. They were numbered between 11024 and 12795. The 365 enginee was identical to that of the 365 2+2 and, in spite of the horsepower increase from 300 to 320, top speed remained the same as the 330, but acceleration was improved.

Other than the enlarged engine displacement, body and chassis specifications were the same as the last 330 GTC and GTS.

A road test of a 330 GTS in *Road & Track* reported that the top had been improved over the 275 GTS because of better sealing around the windows; and the editors were impressed with the ease of putting the top up or down, but they still commented about the wind noise at speed. They were impressed with the seats, both for comfort and adjustment, but weren't happy with the slow electric window lifts that are typical of European-style window mechanisms.

Performance had improved somewhat over the 275 as they recorded 14.9 seconds for the standing-start quarter mile, with a top speed of 95 miles per hour. High praise was given to the engine and suspension (improved since its first use on the 275 GTB and GTS), but the disc brakes needed to be warmed-up before they performed satisfactorily.

This series, both coupe and convertible, is the epitome of style and class for its time period. These cars have all the Ferrari attributes except that they are elegantly restrained. They are for the the person who wants a Ferrari, but doesn't need to tell the world he owns one. Maybe he's a bit smug about his own good taste; he's made it, he knows it, but doesn't care whether anyone else knows it or not.

Introduced at the Geneva auto show in March 1966, the 330 GTC is (in the author's opinion) the best Ferrari road car built. The Pininfarina bodywork is handsome and well finished; it has excellent performance, and with its creature comforts (air conditioning and electric windows were available, and the radio or tape could be heard and appreciated because of the quiet interior) it is a civilized GT car. *Batchelor*

The 330 GTS is a convertible version of the GTC, with all the same amenities plus a folding top for open-air motoring. It is a bit noisier than the coupe, but is still an excellent GT car.

Instrument panel of the 330 GTS is virtually identical to the GTC. This one shows air-conditioning outlets in the console, with window lift buttons on either side of the cigarette lighter (bottom) but no radio. *Gordon Chittenden/Road & Track*

330 GTC and GTS

Engine

Type: . . . . .Colombo-designed, 60-degree V-12
Bore x stroke, mm/inches: 77x71, 3.03x2.79
Displacement, cc/cubic inches: 3957/242
Valve operation: . . . . .Single overhead camshaft on each
  bank with roller followers and rocker arms to inclined valves
Compression ratio: 8.8:1
Carburetion: . . . . .Three Weber twin-choke, downdraft
Bhp (Mfr): . . . . .300 @ 7000

Chassis & drivetrain

Clutch: . . . . .Single dry-plate
Transmission: . . . . .Five-speed, all-synchromesh,
  in unit with the differential, all indirect gears
Rear suspension: . . . . . . .Independent with unequal-length A-arms,
  coil springs, and telescopic shock absorbers
Axle ratio: 3.44:1
Front suspension: . . . . .Independent with unequal-length
  A-arms, coil springs, and telescopic shock absorbers
Frame: . . . . .Welded tubular steel, ladder type

General

Wheelbase, mm/inches: 2400/94.5
Track, front, mm/inches: 1401/55.2
  rear, mm/inches: 1417/55.8
Brakes: . . . . .Disc
Tire size, front and rear: 205-14
Wheels: . . . .*Campagnolo alloy
Body builder: . . . . .Pininfarina
*Borrani wire wheels opitonal.

Either Campagnolo alloy or Borrani wire wheels were available and the buyer's only other option was open or closed bodywork. *Gordon Ghittenden/Road & Track*

Chapter 14

275 GTB/4 and GTS/4
NART Spyder 1966-68
Serial Nos 9323GT - 11069GT
★★★★ GTB/4
★★★★★ GTS/4 NART

275 GTB/4 and GTS/4 NART Spyder 1966-68

Almost exactly two years after the introduction of the 275 GTB, a highly revised edition appeared at the Paris show in 1966. The new car, the 275 GTB/4, looked nearly identical to the 275 GTB, and most mechanical components were the same. The difference was new cylinder heads with dual overhead cams. In this form it produced 300 bhp at 8000 rpm.

As in the latest single-cam 275s, the power was transmitted from the engine to the five-speed transaxle via a torque tube. Suspension was still independent all around with the now ubiquitous unequal-length A-arms, concentric tubular shocks with coil springs, and disc brakes.

A slight bulge in the hood was the only visual difference between the sohc and dohc versions and, unlike the single-cam, no competition model was forthcoming from Ferrari.

The 275 GTB, in 1964, had been the first Ferrari road car to have all-independent suspension; and this new model was the first Ferrari road car to have a double-overhead-camshaft engine. All had six Webers.

At the instigation of Luigi Chinetti, Jr., son of the American Ferrari distributor, a special version of the 275 four-cam was produced in 1967. This was a cabriolet, built by Scaglietti from the basic 275 GTB body shell, and called the NART (for Chinetti's North American Racing Team) Spyder. Only ten cars were built in this configuration, and all were sold by Chinetti in the United States.

The NART Spyder is a beautiful car, and one to be coveted. Approximately 280 of the 275 GTB/4s were built, but the exclusivity of only 10 NART Spyders can't be overlooked.

There was no performance difference between the GTB/4 and GTS/4, and the desirability comes down to personal choice - but as an investment, the open car has to take precedence over the berlinetta.

In a road test of the NART Spyder, *Road & Track* (September 1967 issue) gave the top speed at 155 and the speed at the end of a 14.7-second standing-start quarter mile as 99 miles per hour. I seem to remember Joe Parkhurst's 275 GTB doing the quarter mile at Carlsbad Raceway in a bit over fourteen seconds with a top speed of 102 miles per hour. This was with Joe alone in the car, timed by the raceway's clocks. Most magazine road tests, including the one in *Road & Track*, are done with two in the car and assorted test equipment on board. The weight difference could cause the speed difference.

The "4-cams" don't have the top speed of the later Daytona, but because of their smaller dimensions and lighter weight, they are just as quick in most circumstances. The superb balance and excellent power make them a delight to drive, and there isn't much, if anything, on the road that a 275 GTB/4 driver would have to give way to.

Jean-Pierre Beltoise, the well-known French Grand Prix driver, conducted a road test of a 275 GTB/4 for l'*Auto Journal*, and reported covering forty-six miles in twenty-three minutes on a Sunday afternoon, in spite of "stopping for the tollgates." That's motoring!

The 275 GTB/4 was the first road Ferrari to be powered by a double-poverhead-camshaft engine. It was shown for the first time at the 1966 Paris auto show. Strangely, no competition version was built, as with the single-camshaft 275. *Ferrari*

The 275 GTB/4 was introduced at the Paris show in 1966 (this photo is from the Frankfurt show in 1967).

The visual difference between the two-cam and the four-cam was the hood bulge of the 275 GTB/4. *Molter*

275 GTB/4 and GTS/4 NART Spyder

Engine

Type: . . . . .Colombo-based, 60-degree V-12
Bore x stroke, mm/inches: 77x58.8/3.050x2.315
Displacement, cc/cubic inches: 3286/200.5
Valve operation: . . . . .Double overhead camshafts on each
   bank with cups and spacers operating directly on inclined valves
Compression ratio: 9.2:1
Carburetion: . . . . .Six Weber twin-choke, downdraft
Bhp (Mfr): . . . . .300 @ 8000

Chassis & drivetrain

Clutch: . . . . .Single dry-plate
Transmission: . . . . . . .Five-speed, all-synchromesh, in unit with the
   differential, all indirect gears
Rear suspension: . . . . . . .Independent with unequal-length A-arms,
   coil springs, and telescopic shock absorbers
Axle ratio: 3.55:1
Front suspension: . . . . .Independent with unequal-length
   A-arms, coil springs, and telescopic shock absorbers
Frame: . . . . .Welded tubular steel, ladder type

General

Wheelbase, mm/inches: 2400/94.5
Track, front, mm/inches: 1401/55.2
   rear, mm/inches: 1417/55.8
Brakes: . . . . .Disc
Tire size, front and rear: 205-14
Wheels: . . . . .Campagnolo alloy
Body builder: . . . . .Scaglietti (Pininfarina design)

Luigi Chinetti, Jr., conceived the idea for an open version of the GTB/4 and Scaglietti obliged by creating this handsome model called the NART Spyder. Starting with number 09437, ten NART Spyders were built, and all sold in the United States. *Stan Rosenthal/Road & Track*

The 275 GTB/4 (10351GTB/4) had six Weber carburetors, four overhead camshafts — two per bank
— and dry sump lubrication. *Batchelor*

Chapter 15

365 GTB/4 Daytona 1968-73

365 GTB/4 Daytona
1968-73
Serial Nos. 11795-17081
★★★ 1/2 coupe
★★★★1/2 convertible

At the Paris Salon in October 1968, the new Ferrari 365 GTB/4 was displayed. At that time it was the most expensive (at just under $20,000) and fastest (the factory claim of 174 miles per hour was verified in 1970 by a *Road & Track* road test) road car in the company's twenty-one-year history. It also did 107.5 miles per hour at the end of the standing-start quarter mile which was covered in 13.8 seconds.

Like the 275 GTB which preceded it, the 365 had independent suspension—unequal-length A-arms with concentric tubular shock absorbers and coil springs—both front and rear and Dunlop ventilated disc brakes all around. A welded tubular steel frame tied the two ends together.

The 365 engine was a double-overhead-camshaft V-12, displacing 4.4 liters and, with its six Weber carburetors, produced 352 horsepower at 7500 rpm. Drive went through a five-speed transmission in unit with the differential.

The prototype shown at Paris was designed and built by Pininfarina, but when the Daytona, as the motoring press had dubbed it, went into production a year later, it was once again Scaglietti who built it. And, once again, the bodies were in steel with hood, doors, and trunk lid in aluminum.

When driving the Daytona, one gets the feeling that it is heavy; and at 3,600-plus pounds, it is one of the heaviest cars to come from the Ferrari drawing boards—particularly considering it is only a two-place car.

But the weight doesn't seem to bother handling, and the excellent horsepower and torque give the Daytona performance to match its looks.

When the Daytona first appeared, enthusiasts and journalists seemed divided about its appearance. Nearly three decades later, those who liked it love it; and those who didn't like it, do so now. It is an aggressive-looking design that has features later found on many other European cars.

A year after its debut in Paris, a convertible version, the 365 GTS/4, was exhibited at the Frankfurt show. Ultimately more than 1,300 Daytonas were sold, mostly berlinettas. During the eighties, there were several shops converting berlinettas into cabriolets for their customers. Some of this came about from a genuine desire to drive an open car and some of it from the hope that it would increase the value. For a while it did, but these conversions bring nowhere near what factory convertibles do.

The Daytonas were successfully raced, in spite of their weight penalty. Performance, from acceleration to top speed, was excellent, as was handling. The major weakness of the Daytona in competition was its brakes. This was a result of repeated use of the brakes to slow a tremendously fast car (nearly 200 miles per hour at Le Mans in racing trim) that was also heavy. This would not be a problem for road use. What might be a problem to some buyers would be the relatively heavy steering—particularly at slower speeds. I suggest you drive a Daytona in city traffic before putting your money on the line.

As the last of the great front-engined V-12 berlinettas (until the 456 GT), the Daytona holds a special charm for Ferrari enthusiasts. In many ways it is the most "macho" of all the Ferraris, and its popularity is reflected in its price. The Daytona is an outstanding automobile, and is one of the most desirable Ferraris.

Shown here are two views of one of the Daytona prototypes with its slender spoke "five star" wheels and close-set tail pipes. Unlike other high-performance Ferraris, the Daytona rear was truncated but had no spoiler. *Pininfarina*

Harrah's 365 GTB/4 was a European version with headlights covered by clear plastic, and equipped with wire wheels at the owner's request. A 1970 *Road & Track* road test saw 180 miles per hour indicated at 7000 rpm in fifth gear, which corrected out to 173 miles per hour. *Batchelor*

365 GTB/4 Daytona

Engine

Type: . . . . .Colombo-based, 60-degree V-12
Bore x stroke, mm/inches: 81x71/3.19x2.79
Displacement, cc/cubic inches: .4390/268
Valve operation: . . . . .Double overhead camshafts on each bank with cups and spacers operating directly on inclined valves
Compression ratio: *8.8:1
Carburetion: . . . . .Six Weber twin-choke, downdraft
Bhp (Mfr): . . . .*352 @ 7500

Chassis & drivetrain

Clutch: . . . . .Single dry-plate
Transmission: . . . . .Five-speed ZF, all-synchromesh, in unit with the differential, all indirect gears
Rear suspension: . . . . . . .Independent with unequal-length A-arms, coil springs, and telescopic shock absorbers
Axle ratio: *3.30:1
Front suspension: . . . . . . .Independent with unequal-length A-arms, coil springs, and telescopic shock absorbers
Frame: . . . . .Welded tubular steel, ladder type

General

Wheelbase, mm/inches: 2400/94.5
Track, front, mm/inches: 1490/58.7
rear, mm/inches: 1475/58.1
Brakes: . . . . .Disc
Tire size, front and rear: *215/70-15
Wheels: . . . .*Cromadora alloy
Body builder: . . . . .Scaglietti (Pininfarina design)
*Competition Daytonas had 9.3:1 compression ratio, 405 bhp @ 7500, various axle ratios for different circuits and 10.0/11.0-15 tires. Borrani wire wheels were available on road cars.

The 365 GTB/4 engine was first seen in the United States on a stand at the New York auto show in April 1969. The emission equipment on this engine is not on the European version.

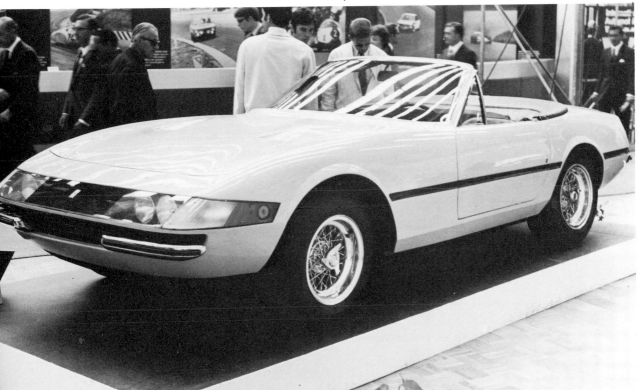

A convertible version, the 365 GTS/4, made its debut at the Frankfurt auto show in October 1969. Not many were made, and quite a few berinettas were rebuilt into cabriolets. Beware of any conversion.

Posh is the word for the Daytona interior. Unfortunately, the seats have no back adjustment; you have to hope you fit. *Hans Tanner*

To comply with United States low, the Pininfarina-bodied Ferrari 365 GTB/4 used retracting sealed-beam headlamps, controlled electrically and also manually in case of emergency. The plexiglass band on the older model was body color on the later cars. The new car was shown at Geneva. *Pininfarina*

The competition 365GTB4A raced successfully at Daytona, LeMans, Watkins Glen, and the Tour de France; and less successfully at Sebring and Spa-Francorchamps. This car (15685GTB4A) finished sixth overall and second in class at Le Mans in 1972, sixth overall and first in class at Watkins Glen the same year, and was sixth overall at Daytona in 1976. *Batchelor*

Filling the engine compartment completely is this European specification 365 four-camshaft engine. The car was Bill Harrah's personal conveyance. *Batchelor*

Chapter 16

365 GTC/4 1971-72

After the 365 GTC was phased out, Ferrari was left without a two-place deluxe tourer until a new model, the 365 GTC/4, was shown at the Geneva show in March 1971. This two-place coupe, with body by Pininfarina, actually had two small seats in the back, but Ferrari realistically didn't describe the car as a 2+2.

The chassis had a wheelbase of 98.4 inches, which placed it between the berlinetta and 2+2 in length. Mechanically, it was closer to the berlinetta.

The engine used the same lower end as the 365 GTB/4 Daytona, but utilized new heads with six side-draft Weber carburetors feeding into manifolds incorporated in the exhaust cam covers. The resultant engine was considerable wider than the Daytona engine but was also lower, allowing a low, sloping hood design. This was the first Ferrari engine created expressly for the U.S. market since stringent controls were placed on emission levels. The five-speed transmission was mounted in unit with the engine.

Enough power was available, even though the American version was slightly detuned from the European non-emission engines (320 and 340 horseower respectively),

to give excellent performance. Once again, though Ferrari brochures quoted weight as 3,190 pounds, a *Road & Track* road test gave weight as 3,825.

Suspension was independent all around with the now common-to-Ferraris unequal-length A-arms and coil springs wound around tubular shock absorbers. Disc brakes were also standard, as was ZF power steering, both of which were necessary for the heavy car.

As the replacement for the 330/365 GTC series, the GTC/4 continued the refinement and luxury that was now expected and received in Ferraris. Air conditioning and a good radio were also included.

In spite of the heavy weight caused by the all-steel body, loads of accessories, and generally large dimensions, the "4" was still an excellent road car with the good manners expected of a GT car from Ferrari. The appearance is one of personal taste, I suppose. It's difficult to fault it on a strictly objective level, yet I feel it doesn't have the charisma of, say, one of the berlinettas, a cabriolet, or even the previous GTC series.

Regardless, it was, and is, a civilized Grand Touring car in the Ferrari style.

Headlights pop up from compartments above the grille; twin hood vents allow exit of hot air from radiator. *Pininfarina*

The sidedraft Webers made the 365 GTC/4 engine lower but wider than the similar unit in the Daytona. The Daytona's dry sump lubrication system was not carried over.

Super clean, but not very exciting, lines mark the 365 GTC/4. Large glass area gives excellent visibility. *Pininfarina*

365 GTC/4

Engine

Type: . . . . .Colombo-based, 60-degree V-12
Bore x stroke, mm/inches: 81x71/3.19x2.79
Displacement, cc/cubic inches: 4390/267.8
Valve operation: . . . . .Double overhead camshafts on each
   bank with cups and spacers operating directly on inclined valves
Compression ratio: 8.8:1
Carburetion: . . . . .Six Weber twin-choke, downdraft
Bhp (Mfr): . . . . .320 @ 6200

Chassis & drivetrain

Clutch: . . . . .Single dry-plate
Transmission: . . . . . .Five-speed, all-synchromesh, all indirect gears
Rear suspension: . . . . .Independent with unequal-length
   A-arms, coil springs, tubular shock absorbers, and antiroll bar
Axle ratio: 4.09:1
Front suspension: . . . . .Independent with unequal-length
   A-arms, coil springs, tubular shock absorbers, and antiroll bar
Frame: . . . . .Welded tubular steel

General

Wheelbase, mm/inches: 2500/98.4
Track, front, mm/inches: 1478/58.2
   rear, mm/inches: 1478/58.2
Brakes: . . . . .Disc
Tire size, front and rear: 215/70-15
Wheels: . . . . .Cromadora alloy
Body builder: . . . . .Pininfarina

Tool kit is shown in trunk compartment that, for Ferrari, is rather spacious. More luggage could be accommodated behind the seats. *Road & Track*

Enormous console was dictated by the forward placement of the seats and the transmission, which is attached to the engine rather than at the rear axle, as on other contemporary Ferraris. *Road & Track*

Typical of most late-model Ferraris, the 365 GTC/4 could be equipped with either alloy or these wire tires. The clean lines are reminiscent of the Daytona, but the chassis is more like the 365 2+2. *Pininfarina and Road & Track*

Chapter 17

365 GT4 BB
1974-76

Note: These cars are all "Gray Market" vehicles in the U.S. Ferrari never produced "Federal versions" of the 365BB. Be certain of the correct title and federal compliance documentation when contemplating buying one of these cars.

Ferrari's first flat, opposed engine was built in 1964. It was a twelve-cylinder, 1.5 liter Formula 1 engine with 11:1 compression ration, Lucas fuel injection, and developed 210 horsepower at 11,000 rpm. An opposed engine is often called a "boxer" engine because of the pistons' reciprocating movement (back and forth, toward and away from each other). The term was originally German, applied to the early VWs and Porsches.

Several other competition Ferraris, both sports and Grand Prix, were built with boxer engines, but the first customer road car with this type of engine was shown at the Turin show in October 1971. It finally went into production in 1973 as the 365 GT4 BB (for 365 Grand Rouring, four-cam Berlinetta Boxer). The 4.4-liter engine was mounted behind the driver and ahead of the rear axle; the first mid-engined Ferrari production car. This is discounting the Dino, which wasn't called a Ferrari.

The main body structure was steel, with the front hood, doors, and rear deck lid (actually the engine cover) made of aluminum, and the lower body panels constructed of fiberglass. The bodies were assembled in Modena by Scaglietti, and no matter what the main body color, the lower panels were matte black.

Suspension was independent all around; with unequal-length A-arms, coil springs, tubular shock absorbers, and antiroll bars front and rear. The prototype had round-and oval-section steel tubing for the frame, but when the boxer went into production, the frame tubes were square and rectangular in cross section—for easier fabrication.

This engine had two toothed-belt-driven overhead camshafts (also a first for Ferrari) on each bank, with intake ports on the lower side. Four, three-throat Weber carburetors fed into twelve ports. The rods and valve gear were interchangeable with the 365 GTC/4.

The boxer's clutch is stiff, and the gated shift lever takes some practice before smooth starts can be made. Acceleration is good but not outstanding (the boxer weighs 3,420 pounds). A road test in 1975 (*Road & Track*) recorded 0-1/4 mile in 15.5 seconds with an end-of-quarter speed at 102.5 miles per hour.

Handling is great for the enthusiast driver. The steering, which is heavy at low speeds, lightens up as speed increases and the tail-heavy weight distribution (43/57 percent), which would normally cause oversteer, is offset by a suspension with understeer designed into it—resulting in an agile, maneuverable car.

The boxer isn't as practical as the Daytona. Both passenger accommodation and luggage space suffer, but is is doubtful if any road-going "customer" Ferrari of the future will have the performance, pizzazz, or sheer animal magnetism of the 365 GT4 BB.

Low engine height of the flat-12 is obvious here with the rear-hinged deck up. Note the roof bracing tubes behind the rear screen. *Batchelor*

The 365 GT4 BB engine marked the first use of a flat, opposed boxer engine in a Ferrari road car. The four overhead camshafts are driven by toothed belts, as on the 308 V-8 engine. Horsepower was quoted as 380 at 7200 rpm. *Ferrari S.P.A.*

Instrument panel of the 365 GT4 BB is functional, but not as attractive as seen in most Ferraris. The panel is covered with a non-glare material resembling newborn mousehide. *Batchelor*

Twin air cleaners cover the four Weber three-choke carburetors. *Batchelor*

365 GT4 BB (Boxer)

Engine

Type: . . . . .Forghieri-based, flat (opposed) 12
Bore x stroke, mm/inches: 81x71/3.19x2.79
Displacement, cc/cubic inches: 4390/267.8
Valve operation: . . . . .Double overhead camshafts on each
    bank with cups and spacers operating directly on inclined valves
Compression ratio: 8.8:1
Carburetion: . . . . .Four Weber three-choke, downdraft
Bhp (Mfr): . . . . .380 DIN @ 7200

Chassis & drivetrain

Clutch: . . . . .Single dry-plate
Transmission: . . . . .Five-speed, all-synchromesh
Rear suspension: . . . . .Independent with unequal-length
    A-arms, coil springs, and telescopic shock absorbers
Axle ratio: . . . . .3.90, 3.75, or 3.46:1
Front suspension: . . . . . . .Independent with unequal-length A-arms,
    coil springs, and telescopic shock absorbers
Frame: . . . . .Welded tubular steel, with aluminum skin

General

Wheelbase, mm/inches: 2500/98.4
Track, front, mm/inches: 1500/59.1
    rear, mm/inches: 1510/59.5
Brakes: . . . . .Disc
Tire size, front and rear: 215/70 VR-15
Wheels: . . . . .Cromadora alloy
Body builder: . . . . .Scaglietti (Pininfarina design)

If any car looks as though it's going 200 miles per hour while standing still, the Boxer is it. The model isn't a practical touring car, but performance and pizzazz make it all worthwhile. *Batchelor*

Chapter 18

512 BB 1976-84
★★

512 BB 1967-84

Note: Ferrari never produced a 512BB for the U.S. market. Any example found here has been "Federalized" by one of several private companies who performed this type of conversion. Most of these companies no longer exist. Many of these cars will no longer comply with current emission regulations in many states. Check carefully before you buy.

In late 1976, a 512 BB was announced as a replacement for the 365 GT4 BB. Superficially, the two cars looked the same, but closer examination reveals the "chin spoiler" (or air dam) under the front grille of the 512, NACA ducts on the lower body sides in front of the rear wheel openings, four taillights instead of six, and the rear body length had been increased by four centimeters (about one and a half inches).

Displacement was increased to 4942 cc (up from 4390) by a bore increase of one millimeter and an increase in the stroke of seven millimeters. Horsepower, however, was down from 380 to 360 DIN, but was achieved at 6200 instead of 7000 rpm. With this engine, Ferrari had come back to his Dino-style nomenclature, with 512 representing the five-liter, twelve-cylinder; while the previous boxer was a 365, representing the displacement of one cylinder.

The Boxers are fantastic cars to drive, with little *raison d'être* other than the sheer pleasure of driving the ultimate sporting GT car. Both passenger and luggage accommodation are minimal, and with the engine just behind the cockpit, the noise is, well, bear-

able, but not conducive to quiet touring.

In other words, you'll get tremendous enjoyment from driving a Boxer, but don't plan a trip greater than a few hundred miles if it is necessary to take anything with you other than a traveling companion. And that should be someone who enjoys the car as much as you do.

512 BB

Engine
Type: . . . . .Forghieri-based, flat (opposed) 12
Bore x stroke, mm/inches: 82x78/3.23x3.07
Displacement, cc/cubic inches: 4942/302.0
Valve operation: . . . . .Double overhead camshafts on each bank, with cups and spacers operating directly on inclined valves
Compression ratio: 9.2:1
Carburetion: . . . . .Four Weber three-choke, downdraft
Bhp (Mfr): . . . . .360 DIN @ 6200
Chassis & drivetrain
Clutch: . . . . .Multi disc
Transmission: . . . . .Five-speed, all-synchromesh
Rear suspension: . . . . .Independent with unequal-length A-arms, coil springs, and telescopic shock absorbers
Axle ratio: 3.21:1
Front suspension: . . . . .Independent with unequal-length A-arms, coil springs, and telescopic shock absorbers
Frame: . . . . .Welded tubular steel, with aluminum skin
General
Wheelbase, mm/inches: 2500/98.4
Track, front, mm/inches: 1500/59.1
rear, mm/inches: 1563/61.5
Brakes: . . . . .Disc
Tire size, front and rear: . . . . .215/70 and 225/70 VR-15
Wheels: . . . . .Cromadora alloy
Body builder: . . . . .Scaglietti (Pininfarina design)

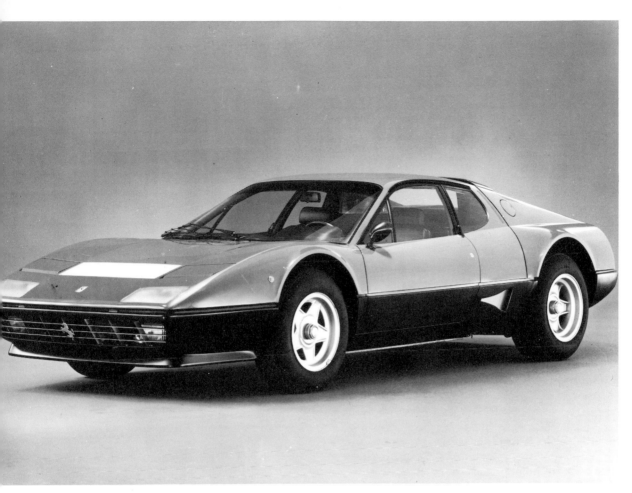

The 512 BB can be distinguished from the 365 GT4 BB by the chin spoiler in front, wider wheels and larger tires, the NACA air intake on the side, and the four taillights at the rear. *Pininfarina*

Testarossa 1985 -
★★★   Testarossa
★★★   512TR
★★★   512M

Chapter 19

Testarossa 1985–91
512TR 1992–96
512M 1995-96

The Testarossa was introduced to the public at the 1984 Paris auto show, and went into production in 1985. It was the first Ferrari created for the American market—at least since safety and emission laws became a fact of life in America. The Testarossa's predecessor, the 512 BB, was never equipped for the American market at the factory, although a few cars arrived in America on the gray market with U.S. conversions to meet U.S. requirements.

The Testarossa body design was by Pininfarina, as was the 512, but the Testarossa was also built by Pininfarina, rather than by Scaglietti. The body was aluminum, with the exception of the roof and doors, which were steel. Pininfarina's wind tunnel was used extensively to develop the shape, with special attention to downforce at both front and rear, possibly even to a slight detriment of the overall drag coefficient which is said to be about 0.36.

A major change in the Testarossa was that two radiators, one on either side of the body, were mounted behind the cockpit with the air intakes extending forward almost to the front of the doors. The long intake trough was found to be necessary after wind tunnel testing.

This radiator placement eliminated a major complaint from 512 owners who didn't like the heat generated by the radiator-to-engine water pipes going alongside the passenger area. The horizontal "slats," which some have called "cheese slicers," were added because some countries require an opening of this size to be protected by some sort of grillework. The rear radiator placement also increased the front luggage space.

The Testarossa engine was an improved 512 design, with the same bore, stroke, displacement, and horizontally-opposed cylinder layout, but with four valve-per-cylinder heads, Marelli's new Multiplex ignition, and Bosch K-Jetronic injection. Horsepower was up to 380 at 5750 rpm, a twenty-horsepower increase over the 512, but enlarged one inch to 9.5 inches in diameter; a necessity because of the 362 foot-pounds of torque at 4500 rpm.

All 1991 Testarossas were forty-nine-state cars, virtually unchanged from the 1990 fifty-state cars. The California Air Research Board refused to exempt the car, as Ferrari was unable to install onboard diagnosis (California OBD) because of its separate fuel and engine management systems. Ferrari replaced the Testarossa in 1992 with the 512TR, once again, a fifty-state car. Between the 1991 and 1992 versions, nearly 85 percent of the vehicle was new, including the arrival of Bosch's Motronic 2.7 integrated electronic ignition/injection system (with California OBD1). This was a great solution when the system behaved itself.

Compression was increased slightly for 1992, to 9.3:1. Maximum horsepower (390) remained the same, but it arrived at a somewhat slower engine speed of 6000 rpm. Its factory-rated top speed rose incrementally as well, to 180.2 mph while road holding benefited from the change to 255/50 VR16 rear tires (fronts remained 225/50 VR16 carried over from the

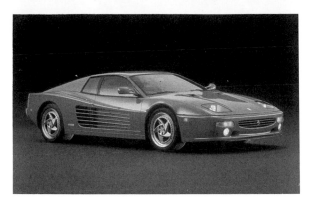

The final version of the Testarossa and 512 body style is this 1995 model year 512M. Still easily recognizable from the side, its front end is cleaned up aerodynamically, gaining considerably from the work that went into developing the F40. The 512M forces 432 hp (SAE) out of the flat-twelve 5.0-liter engine. Ferrari quotes a top speed of 196 mph for the 3,208-pound (dry weight) coupe.

Testarossa). It's hard to believe, but Ferrari quoted fuel economy figures at 55 miles per hour of 30.1 miles per gallon. Of course, even in the days of strictly enforced national limits, who can imagine going only 55 mph in a 512TR? With the Bosch Motronic 2.7 and other internal engine changes, horsepower jumped to 421 at 6750 rpm. This was capable of propelling the car to a factory-quoted top speed of 192 miles per hour with 0-to-100 kilometers per hour coming in 4.8 seconds.

The final, most potent evolution of the car arrived in 1995, the M version—M standing for "modificato," or modified. Modifications to this car amounted to another 35 percent over what was changed from the Testarossa to the first 512TR. Overall, the body remained recognizable but the nose of the car is noticeably different. Ellipsoidal headlights replaced those intrusions into the Pininfarina skin caused by the earlier retractable lights and better air-intake management lessened the grille area.

A single-plate clutch (9.84-inch diameter) replaced the previous twin-plate system. Engine compression increased again, this time to 10.4:1, and power output followed proportionally, to 432 horsepower at 6750 rpm. Four valves per cylinder operated at an included angle of 41 degrees, using new, variable-pitch valve springs derived from racing applications and capable of 10,000-rpm operation, which, as Ferrari's catalog stated, "is well beyond the reachable limits." The published reachable limit of speed was 196 miles per hour. One other important limit to know is that only seventy-five cars were available for the U.S. market.

Testarossa

Engine

Type: . . . . .Flat (opposed) 12
Bore x stroke, mm/inches: 82x78/3.23x3.07
Displacement, cc/cubic inches: 4942/302
Valve operation: . . . . .Double overhead camshafts on each
    bank, with cups and spacers operating directly on inclined
    valves. Four valves per cylinder
Compression ratio: 8.7:1
Carburetion: .Bosch K-Jetronic fuel injection
Bhp (Mfr): . . . . .390 @ 6800

Chassis & drivetrain

Clutch: . . . . .Double-disc dry-plate
Transmission: . . . . .Five-speed, all-synchromesh, all indirect
Rear suspension: . . .Unequal-length A-arms, dual coil springs, dual
tubular shock absorbers, antiroll bar
Axle ratio: 3.21:1
Front suspension: . . . . .Unequal-length A-arms, coil springs,
    tubular shock absorbers, antiroll bar
Frame: . . . . .Welded tubular steel

General

Wheelbase, mm/inches: .2550/100.4
Track, front, mm/inches: .1518/59.8
    rear, mm/inches: 1660/65.4
Brakes: . . . . .Disc
Tire size, front and rear: . . . .Goodyear Eagle VR50, 225/50 VR-16
Wheels: . . . . .Cast-alloy, 16x8J front, 16x10J rear
Body builder & Designer: . . . . .Pininfarina

Chapter 20

410 Superamerica
I, II, and III 1956 - 59
Serial Nos. 0423SA - 1495SA
★★★★

410 Superamerica I, II and III 1956-59

The 410 Superamerica with Pinin Farina bodywork was introduced to the public at the Brussels auto show in February 1956. The chassis and engine had been seen at the Paris Salon in October 1955.

This series of Ferraris was built in three groups: fifteen cars with serial numbers 0423SA to 0497SA, all on a 110.2 inch wheelbase and all with Pinin Farina bodies except for one Ghia coupe and a coupe and convertible with Boano bodywork; eight more with a 102.3-inch wheelbase and all with Farina bodies, serial numbers 0499SA to 0721SA; and, in 1959, a third series with numbers between 1015SA and 1495SA, still on the 102.3-inch chassis and with Pinin Farina bodies.

Some of the Superamericas looked alike, but all were decidedly custom, one-of-a-kind cars. No two 410s were exactly the same.

The 410s were also big and heavy, as GT cars go. Ferrari specifications are generally pretty accurate, except for weight figures, which seem to be selected in some mysterious way totally unrelated to reality. The 410 supposedly weighed under 3,000 pounds, but a *Road & Track* road test in 1962 gave the curb weight (obtained at a certified public weigh station) as 3,550 pounds.

All this mass is propelled by a powerful engine of 340-400 bhp, depending on whose figures you read, driving through a multiple-disc clutch. The 410 in Harrah's Automobile Collection was converted to a single dry-plate clutch. This makes the car much easier to drive, but the clutch is unable to handle the torque, and considerable clutch slippage results if the driver is the least bit careless. A four-speed transmission is used on all 410s.

Clutches are probably the weakest link in Ferrari's drivetrain. The standard procedure is to very gently apply throttle pressure as the clutch is released. After the clutch is fully engaged, any amount of throttle can be applied without too much fear of slippage. Drag-race starts are not recommended for any Ferrari, and if used will soon destroy the clutch. In spite of a marginal clutch, *Road & Track* achieved a quarter-mile time of 14.6 seconds and 101 miles per hour.

Handling and ride characteristics of the Superamerica reflect its large dimensions and weight, but this will probably be more obvious to someone familiar with other Ferraris than it would be to someone experiencing his first Ferrari drive.

Though their styling and handling are dated, their build quality was superb. Many of the 410s survive to this day in original condition. These are some of Ferrari's most spectacular machines and their individuality enhances their value. The Superamerica was built for cross-country touring, to cover long distances at high speeds with disconcerting ease. These are perfect cars for Montana's Interstates.

Mario Boano built two 410 Superamerica bodies, this coupe (0477SA) and a similar convertible (0485SA), in 1956. Boano seemed to be more influenced by Detroit than either Turin or Milan. *Moisio/Boano*

Two 1956-57 410 Superamericas with very subtle body differences. Visible are the side vent and windshield/side window trim differences.

While there is a body builder's crest on each car, only the dark-colored one displays the Pinin Farina name. *Pininfarina*

The star of the Pinin Farina stand at the 1956 Paris Salon was this 410 Superfast (0483SA) on the new shorter chassis. It was commissioned by California oil-industrialist William Doheny who was also the backer of Ernie McAfee's Ferrari agency in Hollywood. *Ralph Poole*

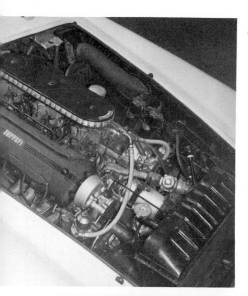

0483 was created as a "showpiece" from the basic 410 SA. A large speedometer and tachometer flanked a dial containing water temperature, fuel, and oil pressure gauges. The twin distributors were so far back in the engine compartment that a cowl door had to be opened (behind the hood) to work on them. *Ralph Poole*

Pinin Farina displayed this 410 Superfast (0719SA) at Turin in 1957. The basic body shape was similar to the 1956 Superfast (0483SA), but looked better without the fins. *Pininfarina*

Instrument panels varied as much as the exteriors, but the (1477SA) is fairly typical of the 410 series cars. *Batchelor*

The trunk of the 1959 410 (1477SA) is large enough for serious travelers. *Batchelor*

410 Superamerica I, II, and III

Engine
Type: .Lampredi-designed, 60-degree V-12
Bore x stroke, mm/inches: 88x68/3.46x2.68
Displacement, cc/cubic inches: 4962/302.7
Valve operation: . . . . .Single overhead camshafts on each
   bank with roller followers and rocker arms to inclined valves
Compression ratio: *8.5:1
Carburetion: . . . . .Three Weber twin-choke, downdrat
Bhp (Mfr): . . . .*340 @ 6000

Chassis & drivetrain
Clutch: . . . . .Multiple disc
Transmission: . . . . .Four-speed, all-synchromesh,
   direct drive in fourth
Rear suspension: . . . . .Live axle with semi-elliptic springs,
   located by parallel trailing arms, and lever-action shock absorbers
Axle ratio: . . . .*3.67, 3.44, 3.22, or 3.11.1
Front suspension: . . . . .Independent with unequal-length
   A-arms, coil springs, and lever-action shock absorbers
Frame: . . . . .Welded tubular steel, ladder type

General
Wheelbase, mm/inches: *2800/110
Track, front, mm/inches: 1455/58.4
   rear, mm/inches: 1450/58.2
Brakes: .Aluminum drums with iron liners
Tire size, front and rear: 6.50-16
Wheels: . . . . .Borrani wire, center-lock, knock-off
Body builder: . . . .*Pinin Farina
*1958-59 models had 9:1 compression ratio, 400 bhp @ 6500 rpm, 2600 mm wheelbase (102.3 inches), and added axle ratios of 4.85, 4.57, 4.25, 3.78, 3.55, and 3.33:1. A few bodies were built by Boano and one was built by Ghia.

In 1958 (top) and 1959 (bottom) there were greater differences; top treatment, side vents, and head- lights being the most noticeable. No two of the 410s were alike. *Pininfarina*

Chapter 21

400 Superamerica
I and II 1960-64
Serial Nos. 1517SA-5139SA
★★★★

400 Superamerica I and II 1960-64

The Brussels show was once again, in February 1960, the public debut of a Ferrari Superamerica—this time, the 400 SA. It was a cabriolet by Pinin Farina, with four liter "small-block" Colombo V-12 engine in its 95.2-inch wheelbase. Production wasn't to get started until 1961, however.

Like the 410 SA that preceded it, the 400 changed wheelbase in mid-run, but this time it got longer, rather than shorter—from 95.2 to 102.3 inches, in 1962.

Also, like the 410, no two 400s were alike. All but two (built by Scaglietti) carried Pinin Farina bodies, but were individually tailored to customers' wishes. This resulted in a series of cars that were generally the same; basic engine and mechanical specs didn't change through the series, but body design and trim could and did.

The Colombo-designed engine had more displacement than any previous small-block version, with a subsequent increase in horsepower. Claims up to 400 bhp were made, and while we know these 400s were fast, it is technically impossible for these customer engines to produce that much power.

A Superamerica, either 410 or 400, was created for the affluent (even more so than your average Ferrari buyer) automobile enthusiast, the customer who wanted to travel in the best possible style which, meant a Ferrari, but not a run-of-the mill Ferrari.

All Ferrari road cars of this period had similar chassis; independent front suspension with coil springs, and live rear axle with semi-elliptic springs and parallel trailing arms for axle location.

With their tremendous torque, slippery bodywork, and heavy weight, these 400 Superamericas needed good brakes. The 400s came with disc brakes, which were far superior to the drum brakes of the 410, but not to modern discs.

Whereas the 410 had a four-speed transmission, the 400 had a four-speed plus overdrive. Fourth is direct and overdrive is a step-up ratio of 28.2 percent.

As always, the Pinin Farina bodywork was not only handsome, but well finished. Traveling in a Superamerica was traveling in style. The owners knew it, and all who saw the car knew it, which is what the owners wanted them to know. Isn't that generally the idea of driving something different?

The body design of most Superamericas has worn well, and they still look great today.

After the first Superfast (a 410, built in 1956), Pinin Farina displayed Superfast II (on 400 SA chassis number 2207SA) at Turin in 1960. It had retractable headlights, and no hood scoop. Shortly after, it acquired a hood scoop and vent windows, and the rear skirts were removed (lower photos). *Pininfarina*

Pininfarina also built 400 SA cabriolets: one (3309SA) with covered headlights, and the other (2407SA) with open lights and a removable hardtop. These cars are, at first glance, much like the 250 GT cabriolets by Pinin Farina. *Pininfarina*

---

400 Superamerica I and II (SA)
Engine
Type: . . . . .Colombo-designed, 60-degree V-12
Bore x stroke, mm/inches: 77x71/3.05x2.79
Displacement, cc/cubic inches: 3967/242
Valve operation: . . . . .Single overhead camshafts on each
    bank with roller followers and rocker arms to inclined valves
Compression ratio: *8.8:1
Carburetion: . . . .*Three Weber twin-choke, downdrat
Bhp (Mfr): . . . .*340 @ 7000
Chassis & drivetrain
Clutch: . . . . .Single dry-plate
Transmission: . . . . .Four-speed, all-synchromesh, direct
    drive in fourth with electrically-operated overdrive (28.2%) in fifth
Rear suspension: . . . . .Live axle with semi-elliptic springs,
    located by parallel trailing arms, and lever-action shock absorbers
Axle ratio: . . . .*3.66, 3.78, or 4.00:1

Front suspension: . . . . .Independent with unequal-length
    A-arms, coil springs, and telescopic shock absorbers
Frame: .Welded tubular steel, ladder type
General
Wheelbase, mm/inches: *2600/102.3
Track, front, mm/inches: 1360/53.5
    rear, mm/inches: 1346/53.0
Brakes: . . . . .Disc
Tire size, front and rear: 6.50-15
Wheels: . . . . .Borrani wire, center-lock, knock-off
Body builder: . . . . .Pinin Farina
*Early 400 Sas had 9.8:1 compression ratio, 400 bhp @ 6750 rpm
and shorter wheelbase — 2413 mm/95.2 inches. A few 400 Sas had
Solex carburetors. Two cars had Scaglietti bodies.

A 400 Superamerica Aerodinamico on the short chassis (2861SA) is typical of the series, all of which had Pininfarina bodies except for two by Scaglietti. This was Bill Harrah's car, extensively "hot-rodded" by Bill Rudd after Harrah was humiliated by a Pontiac in a street race. *Batchelor*

Three 400 Superamericas look similar, but there are differences in grilles, parking-light location, hoods, door handles, and one car has an air outlet behind the rear wheel, in the lower fender. *Pininfarina*

In 1962, Superfast II was rebuilt into Superfast IV 400 Superamerica (2207SA). The top configuration was similar but not identical to SFIII. Retracting headlights gave way to quads a la 330 GT 2+2. This car was also shown with—and without—a hood scoop. For years it was believed that there were four cars. In fact, it was all the same car, changed repeatedly by Pininfarina design studio. *Pininfarina*

The 400 SA engine (type 163), shown here in cabriolet 2331SA was the immediate predecessor to the 330 GT's type 209 V-12. The "400" designation stood for four liters, not 400 horsepower. *Paul Swartzel*

This 400 SA cabriolet by Pinin Farina appears, with just a casual look, to be a 250 Spyder California, but compare it to the Spyders in Chapter Five. *Pininfarina*

A few 400s used Solex carburetors and Bosch ignition. Once the rumor started that "400" referred to horsepower, Ferrari let it go, never disputing the myth. These engines were actually in a mild state of tune. *Karl Dedolph*

Superfast III (a variation on chassis number 2207SA) was shown at Geneva in 1963. It had the same headlight treatment as SF II, but added a thermostatically controlled retracting grille cover. *Pininfarina*

Chapter 22

500 Superfast 1964-66

Continuing the luxury image Ferrari had established with the 410 and 400 Superamericas, a new king of the road was shown to an admiring public at the Geneva show in March 1964. This new car was called the 500 Superfast.

Its engine was a 4962 cc V-12 and was unique to this model. The design followed the Colombo practice of having removable cylinder heads, but the dimensions were the same as the Lampredi "long-block" engines of the 410 Superamerica and some of the earlier 250 Europas and 375 Americas.

Other than the engine, mechanical specifications were almost identical to the 330 GT. Drive went through a four-speed transmission, with Laycock de Normanville overdrive, to a live rear axle. Suspension was still independent in front with unequal-length A-arms and coil springs, and the rear axle was supported by semi-elliptic springs and located by parallel trailing arms on each side.

In 1965, the 500 SF underwent running changes that were also being made to the 330 GT 2+2; new engine mounts, suspended pedals, and five-speed transmission replaced the four plus overdrive.

Outside, both the 500 SF and 330 GT received new air outlets for the front fenders, but the basic body remained unchanged throughtout the model run.

---

500 Superfast (SF)

Engine

Type: .Colombo-designed, 60-degree V-12
Bore x stroke, mm/inches: 88x68/3.46x2.68
Displacement, cc/cubic inches: 4962/302.7
Valve operation: . . . . .Single overhead camshafts on each bank with roller followers and rocker arms to inclined valves
Compression ratio: 8.8:1
Carburetion: . . . . .Three Weber twin-choke, downdrat
Bhp (Mfr): . . . . .400 @ 6500

Chassis & drivetrain

Clutch: . . . . .Multiple-disc
Transmission: . . . .*Five-speed, all-synchromesh, direct drive in fourth
Rear suspension: . . . . . .Live axle with semi-elliptic springs, located by parallel trailing arms, with telescopic shock absorbers

Axle ratio: . . . .*Various, according to customer's request
Front suspension: . . . . .Independent with unequal-length A-arms, coil springs, and telescopic shock absorbers
Frame: . . . . .Welded tubular steel, ladder type

General

Wheelbase, mm/inches: *2650/104.2
Track, front, mm/inches: 1407/55.5
rear, mm/inches: 1397/55.2
Brakes: . . . . .Disc
Tire size, front and rear: 6.50-16
Wheels: . . . . .Borrani wire, center-lock, knock-off
Body builder: . . . . .Pininfarina
*Virtually all 11 ratios from 410 and 400 SA, and 365 GT 2+2 available. Four-speed plus overdrive transmission was used in 1964 and early 1965 models.

Production started early in 1964 on the 500 Superfast, which bears a strong resemblance to its predecessor, the 400 SA. The main visual differences are uncovered headlights and squared-off tail of the Superfast. *Pininfarina*

Luxurious interiors of the 500 SF are traditional Ferrari/Pininfarina. The shift lever controls a four-speed engine-mounted transmission with a Bianchi-built Laycock over-drive. Later cars used the five-speed gearbox from the Series II 330 GT 2+2. *Pininfarina and Karl Dedolph*

The 500 Superfast was visually evolutionary from the 400 Superamericas and continued the super-deluxe image of the SAs. The body was almost devoid of decoration, and was totally unprotected from side damage. *Pininfarina*

Chapter 23

365 California
1966 - 67
Serial Nos. 8347-10369
★★★★

365 California 1966-67

The 365 California shared a name with the earlier 250 GT California, but was theoretically a cabiolet successor to the 500 Superfast coupe. The new car was created by the Ferrari/Pininfarina amalgam, which has been so successful over the years, and was unveiled at the 1966 Geneva show.

Power came from a single-overhead camshaft V-12 virtually identical to the 365 GTC and 2+2 engine. The 365 engine in the California had a 4390 cc displacement, 8.8:1 compression ratio, and produced 320 horsepower at 6600 rpm. Drive went through a five-speed transmission like that of the 500 SF and the 330 2+2. Power steering was standard and, unlike its contemporaries, Borrani wire wheels were standard and Campagnolo alloy wheels were optional.

During its one year of production, fourteen examples were built, about half of which came to the United States.

Pininfarina's body design borrowed heavily from other PF designs: the front from the 500 Superfast and the body sides, with air intake surrounding the door handles, from the 246 Dino. The rear, however, was unique to the 365.

This model is not well known, nor was it well received because it is so rare. It is big and heavy, in the tradition of the Superamericas,

365 California

Engine
Type: .Colombo-designed, 60-degree V-12
Bore x stroke, mm/inches: 71x71/3.19x2.79
Displacement, cc/cubic inches: 4390/268
Valve operation: . . . . .Single overhead camshaft on each bank with roller followers and rocker arms to inclined valves
Compression ratio: 8.8:1
Carburetion: . . . . .Three Weber twin-choke, downdraft
Chassis & drivetrain
Clutch: . . . . .Single dry-plate
Transmission: . . . .*Five-speed, all-synchromesh, direct drive in fourth
Rear suspension: . . . . .Live axle with semi-elliptic springs, located by parallel trailing arms, with telescopic shock absorbers
Axle ratio: 4.25:1
Front suspension: . . . . .Independent with unequal-length A-arms, coil springs, and telescopic shock absorbers
Frame: .Welded tubular steel, ladder type
General
Wheelbase, mm/inches: .2650/104.2
Track, front, mm/inches: 1397/55.2
rear, mm/inches: 1389/54.7
Brakes: . . . . .Disc
Tire size, front and rear: 205-15
Wheels: . . . . .Borrani wire, center-lock, knock-off
Body builder: . . . . .Pininfarina

and is classed as one of the "luxury" Ferrari GTs. But, because it is an open car, it is set apart from most other versions of the Ferrari luxury series.

The 365 California's Pininfarina bodywork borrowed its front from the 500 Superfast, and the door handle/air scoop from the 246 Dino. Pop-up driving lights retracted into the nose, just above the hood opening. *Pininfarina*

250 GTE 2+2
1960-63

Several 2+2 bodies were built on Ferrari cars in the early fifties, by Carrozzeria Touring, Ghia, and Vignale, but they were not series-built cars, and the rear passenger accommodation was unacceptable for much more than a trip around the block.

The prototype for the first series production Ferrari 2+2 was used as the course marshal's car at the Le Mans 24-Hour Race in June 1960, which was the first time it had been publicly displayed. Its official debut was at the Paris auto show in October 1960, however. This 2+2 was built on the same 102.3-inch wheelbase chassis used for the two-passenger cars, but the engine had been moved forward eight inches to allow for the needed additional passenger space.

The bodywork, by Pinin Farina, was all-new and, with minor changes, continued to the end of 1963 (the start of the replacement 330 2+2) as the 250 GTE.

Mechanically (other than modifications necessary when the engine was moved forward), the 2+2 was almost identical to the two-passenger contemporary Ferraris. It had independent front suspension with coil springs, semi-elliptic rear springs supporting a live axle positioned by twin parallel trailing arms on each side, telescopic shock absorbers, and disc brakes all around. The transmission was a four-speed with Laycock de Normanville overdrive.

The cylinder heads were now the standard Ferrari units which followed the Testa Rossa pattern with spark plugs on the outside of the heads, individual intake ports, and coil valve springs.

Moving the engine forward was slightly detrimental to handling, as it increased the understeering tendencies. A 2+2 owner was not usually inclined to drive his car as hard as the owner of a two-passenger model, but if he did, the trick was to tweak the steering wheel just a bit going into a corner to break the rear wheels loose, then manage the understeer/oversteer by judicious use of steering and throttle (an easy thing to do with a Ferrari).

The 2+2 doesn't have the pizzazz of some other Ferraris, and it isn't any better or worse mechanically than its contemporaries. But it does offer Grand Touring for a couple with two small children, or four adults can arrive at the theater in grand style without the ladies' clothing being too ruffled.

Late in the 250 2+2 model run in late 1963, about fifty cars were built (between 4953 and 5175) with the then-new 4.0-liter (330 V-12) engine. The only identification on this model to separate it from the 250, is a nameplate on the rear that says AMERICA—and not all of them were so labeled. The 330 engine was the type 209, which is several inches longer than the 250 GT engine.

The GTE and AMERICA are sleepers for investment purposes. Many were cut up for parts or for rebodies as replicars during the late eighties, consequently there are fewer now. They certainly won't appreciate as much as the competition-oriented cars, but as a V-12 Ferrari, they represent excellent value for money.

The prototype 250 GTE 2+2, in 1960 had chrome headlight bezels and louvers behind the quarter windows but no louvers on the front fenders. *Pininfarina*

The second pre-production prototype 250 GT 2+2 had small side reflectors on front fenders, but no louvers. With cleaner side treatment, it is one of the better looking of the series. *Pininfarina*

250 GTE 2+2

Engine

Type: . . . . .Colombo-designed, 60-degree V-12
Bore x stroke, mm/inches: 73x58.8/2.870x2.315
Displacement, cc/cubic inches: 2953/180.0
Valve operation: . . . . .Single overhead camshaft on each
   bank with roller followers and rocker arms to inclined valves
Compression ratio: 8.8:1
Carburetion: . . . . .Three Weber twin-choke, downdraft
Bhp (Mfr) . . . . .240 @ 7000

Chassis & drivetrain

Clutch: . . . . .Single dry-plate
Transmission: . . .Four-speed, all-synchromesh, direct drive in fourth
   with overdrive in fifth (4.57 axle only)
Rear suspension: . . . .Live axle with semi-elliptic springs, located by
   parallel trailing arms, with telescopic shock absorbers

Axle ratio: . . . . .4.57 or 4.25:1
Front suspension: . . . . .Independent with unequal-length
   A-arms, coil springs, and telescopic shock absorbers
Frame: .Welded tubular steel, ladder type

General

Wheelbase, mm/inches: 2600/102.3
Track, front, mm/inches: 1354/53.3
   rear, mm/inches: 1394/54.9
Brakes: . . . . .Disc
Tire size, front and rear: . . . . .6.50-15 or 185-15
Wheels: . . . . .Borrani wire, center-lock, knock-off
Body builder: . . . . .Pinin Farina

The 1961-62 production version had a large chrome area around taillights, front parking lights under the headlights, and driving lights in front of grille. *Batchelor*

You may think that once you've seen one Ferrari engine compartment, you've seen them all, but there are variations; air cleaner height, location of ancillary components, sometimes even component brands. *Batchelor*

Late-1962 and 1963 models had chrome headlight rims again and rearranged parking and driving lights. The taillights were considerably cleaned up as well. *Pininfarina*

Chapter 25

330 GT 2+2
1964 - 68
Serial Nos. 5165GT-10193GT
★★

330 GT 2+2
1964-68

Ferrari holds a press conference early each year in Maranello to display his offerings for the coming year. At his January 1964 press conference, a new four-liter 330 2+2 made its debut and met with decidedly mixed reviews.

The designer/builder was still Pininfarina, but the body was bulbous and, wonder of wonders, had four headlights. The press was enthusiastic while in Ferrari's presence, but once back at their typewriters, they were much less so. Griff Borgeson, writing in *Road & Track* (April 1964) quotes body builder Scaglietti on the new 2+2, "We all panic at every new Pininfarina design, convinced that the public will never accept it . . . But watch the 330 and see how the public likes it a few months from now . . . Pininfarina has an uncanny sense for being right about what the public wants . . . As for things that go, Ing. Ferrari just keeps on pointing the way."

Apparently both Pininfarina and Scaglietti were right, but in 1965, the model did lose two of its headlights, which brought the shape and style closer to what enthusiasts expected from Ferrari and Pininfarina.

Underneath the metal, the chassis was still all Ferrari in style and substance. The wheelbase was lengthened five centimeters, or about two inches, and the driveline was strengthened to absorb the load of the increased horsepower from the four-liter engine. Koni adjustable shock absorbers were used in conjunction with concentric coil helper springs at the rear, as on the Lusso, and a separate front and rear brake system eliminated the possibility of total brake failure.

Running changes in Ferrari mechanical specifications were incorporated into the 330 2+2 in 1965, such as five-speed gearbox, suspended pedals, and making available power steering and air conditioning. Ferrari was truly entering the era of the "family" or daily "go-to-work" car.

All bodywork of both the 250 and 330 2+2 was by Pininfarina and is superior to the two-place cars which are built in smaller quantities, necessitating more handwork. Handwork oftens covers poor panel contour, or fit, so it looks good on the outside but in actual fact is not as well built as a mass-produced body (it won't stand up as well either).

Alloy disc wheels were standard on 330 2+2s, but wire wheels were optional. Both types have advantages and disadvantages. Wire wheels look better on most Ferrari models, but are difficult to keep clean and have to be checked regularly for bent, broken, or loose spokes.

During the four years of production, approximately 1,000 of the 330 2+2s were built, which does make finding one a relatively easy task. Unfortunately, if a 2+2 (250 or 330) needs much engine work, it is just as costly as redoing a more valuable 250 berlinetta or spyder - either of which are better investments, if that is a major consideration.

The first 330 GT 2+2s were actually 250s with 330 engines. These interim cars were called AMERICA and used an entirely new engine, not, as an old ref-erence states, the 3.0-liter engine which had been bored and stroked out to 4.0 liters. *Moncalvo*

To some observers, the Ferrari prancing stallion became a Percheron with the advent of the 330 2+2; but what it gave up in looks, it gained in passenger accommodation. *Pininfarina*

In 1965, the 330 look changed, with the more classic front featuring two headlights instead of four, and new side vents. At this point, the four-speed O/D transmission gave way to a five-speed; alloy wheels became standard with wire wheels optional; and both power steering and air conditioning were available. *Pininfarina*

330 GT 2+2

Engine

Type: . . . . .Colombo-designed, 60-degree V-12
Bore x stroke, mm/inches: 77x71/3.03x2.79
Displacement, cc/cubic inches: 3967/242
Valve operation: . . . . .Single overhead camshaft on each
bank with roller followers and rocker arms to inclined valves
Compression ratio: 8.8:1
Carburetion: . . . . .Three Weber twin-choke, downdraft
Bhp (Mfr) . . . . .300 @ 6600

Chassis & drivetrain

Clutch: . . . . .Single dry-plate
Transmission: . . . .*Four-speed, all-synchromesh,
direct drive in fourth with electrically operated overdrive (22%) in fifth
Rear suspension: . . . . .Live axle with semi-elliptic springs,
located by parallel trailing arms, with telescopic shock absorbers
Axle ratio: 4.25:1
Front suspension: . . . . .Independent with unequal-length
A-arms, coil springs, and telescopic shock absorbers
Frame:. .Welded tubular steel, ladder type

General

Wheelbase, mm/inches: 2650/104.2
Track, front, mm/inches: 1397/55.2
rear, mm/inches: 1389/54.7
Brakes: . . . . .Disc
Tire size, front and rear: 205-15
Wheels: . . . .*Borrani wire, center-lock, knock-off
Body builder: . . . . .Pininfarina
*1966-67 2+2s had five-speed transmissions. In 1965 alloy wheels
became standard and wire wheels were optional.

Chapter 26

365 GT 2+2
1967 - 71
Serial Nos. 10791GT - 14099GT
★★★

365 GT 2+2
1967-71

More than 2,000 of the 250 and 330 GT 2+2s had been produced by Ferrari/Pininfarina in the eight years of their model run, attesting to the desirability of the body style. Buyers of this body type were generally more concerned about creature comforts and space than were the buyers of the two-passenger models, and Ferrari introduced more and more features calculated to attract this buyer.

A new 2+2 was unveiled at the Paris Salon in October 1967, and displayed mechanical features previously not seen on production Ferraris. The new model had full independent suspension (the first 2+2 to be so equipped), concentric Koni telescopic shock absorbers, and coil springs all around, coupled with a Koni and Ferrari-developed self-leveling rear suspension. Power steering and air conditioning were standard equipment.

The chassis was still the typical Ferrari welded-tube arrangement but with the advent of independent rear suspension, drive went through the single-disc dry-plate clutch and five-speed, all synchromesh transmission to the rear axle assembly via a torque tube. This setup was already in use in the 330 GTC and 275 GTB/4; one advantage being that less noise was transmitted to the interior.

Wheelbase of the 365 2+2 was 2650 millimeter (104.3 inches), as on the 330 2+2; but the body had an entirely new look, more reminiscent of the 500 Superfast than of the previous 2+2s. The 365 2+2 is big and heavy when compared to GT cars of the world, but because of its Ferrari heritage, it retains as many of the traditional sporting characteristics as possible.

Some Ferrari historians and researchers will no doubt quarrel with my three-star rating of this car compared with the two previous 2+2s. My reason for this is simply that the 365 was the most sophisticated, most up-to-date state-of-the-art Ferrari produced up to its date of manufacture. It will come closer to giving its passengers a ride quality and comfort level compatible to the eighties than will any of the older model Ferraris—without losing the "Ferrari feel."

The 365 GT 2+2 introduced in 1967 was the first Ferrari 2+2 to have all-independent suspension. It was also the first Ferrari to have a self-leveling rear suspension. *Pininfarina*

Luxurious interior is extremely comfortable for front seat passengers, with plenty of seat travel and back angle adjustment, but when rear passengers are carried, it gets tight. *Pininfarina/Hans Tanner*

Alloy wheels were standard on the 365 2+2, but Borrani wire wheels were optional for the "traditionalist" Ferrari buyer. *Road & Track*

For the U.S.-version engine compartment, Ferrari had to stuff in not only air conditioning and power steering pumps but also the emissions air pump and its plumbing. U.S. cars even carried twin alternators. *Coltrin*

---

365 GT 2+2

Engine

Type: .Colombo-designed, 60-degree V-12
Bore x stroke, mm/inches: 81x71/3.19x2.79
Displacement, cc/cubic inches: .4390/268
Valve operation: . . . . .Single overhead camshaft on each bank with roller followers and rocker arms to inclined valves
Compression ratio: 8.8:1
Carburetion: . . . . .Three Weber twin-choke, downdraft
Bhp (Mfr) . . . . .320 @ 6600

Chassis & drivetrain

Clutch: . . . . .Single dry-plate
Transmission: . . .Five-speed, all-synchromesh, direct drive in fourth
Rear suspension: . . . . . . .Independent with unequal-length A-arms, coil springs, and telescopic shock absorbers (with hydropneumatic leveling device)
Axle ratio: 4.25:1
Front suspension: . . . . .Independent with unequal-length A-arms, coil springs, and telescopic shock absorbers
Frame: . . . . .Welded tubular steel, ladder type

General

Wheelbase, mm/inches: 2650/104.2
Track, front, mm/inches: 1437/56.6
        rear, mm/inches: 1468/57.8
Brakes: . . . . .Disc
Tire size, front and rear: .215/70 VR-15
Wheels: . . . .*Cromadora alloy
Body builder: . . . . .Pininfarina
*Wire wheels optional.

---

Chapter 27

365 GT4 2+2
1972-76

(Note: Ferrari did not produce this model for the U.S. market. Any of these models in the U.S. are "Gray Market" versions. Current emissions regulations require that these cars pass stringent tests. The equipment originally installed to convert them to U.S. federal specifications may have been removed. Beware and check carefully.)

In European terminology, the 365 GT4 2+2 is a coupe, but Americans would more likely refer to it as a two-door sedan, because of its general appearance and interior accommodation. Its wheelbase is two inches longer, but its overall length is seven and one half inches shorter than the 365 2+2 that preceded it.

When this new 2+2 was introduced at the Paris show in 1972, a year and a half had elapsed since production stopped on the 365 2+2, which is unusual for Ferrari; he usually has a replacement ready to go into production before the previous model is dropped.

Mechanically, the new car, the 365 GT4, was like the 365 GTC/4 rather than the 2+2 it was replacing. A four-cam, 4.4 liter V-12 with six horizontal Weber carburetors furnished the power, which went through a five-speed transmission and torque tube to the chassis-mounted differential.

Ferrari specifications, while always interesting and impressive, tend to be similar from model to model (at least for contemporary models from the company), so the main interest in this new 2+2 was in the Farina bodywork.

It was not only on a longer wheelbase and yet shorter overall than its predecessor, but passenger and luggage space had also been enlarged considerably. "Smaller on the outside, larger on the inside" had genuine meaning.

In 1975, Dean Batchelor drove Bill Harrah's personal 365 GT4 from Reno, Nevada, to Monterey, California (for the Historic Car Races and Pebble Beach Concours d'Elegance), and back. The car is heavy. You can tell it by the general feel of the controls and response, but it didn't seem to detract from the enjoyment of the car.

There was more than enough room for two and luggage, and it proved to be comfortable, no matter what the road surface or driving conditions (during the trip he started from 4,500 feet altitude of Reno, went up to 9,000 feet at the top of Mt. Rose Highway and back down to sea level at Monterey).

Dean kept to legal speed limits most of the time, but found that the car could crest the top of Mt. Rose Highway at 90 miles per hour; and this at nearly 9,000 feet altitude, going uphill, on a mildly winding road. Given a straight road the car could easily have topped 100 miles per hour at the summit of the mountain.

This test was unnecessary, of course, but was a lot of fun, and more than satisfied any question about the performance of a car that Ferrari enthusiasts think has been emasculated.

The 365 GT4 2+2 was introduced in 1972 as a replacement for the 365 2+2, but mechanically it was like the 365 GTC/4, with a 20-centimeter-longer wheelbase. *Pininfarina*

---

365 GT4 2+2

Engine

Type: .Colombo-designed, 60-degree V-12
Bore x stroke, mm/inches: 81x71/3.19x2.79
Displacement, cc/cubic inches: 4390/267.8
Valve operation: . . . .Double overhead camshaft on each bank with
  cups and spacers operating directly on inclined valves
Compression ratio: 8.8:1
Carburetion: . . . . .Six Weber twin-choke, sidedraft
Bhp (Mfr) . . . . .320 @ 6200

Chassis & drivetrain

Clutch: . . . . .Single dry-plate
Transmission: . . . . .Five-speed, all-synchromesh,
  direct drive in fourth
Rear suspension: . . . . .Independent with unequal-length

A-arms, coil springs, tubular shock absorbers, and antiroll bar
Axle ratio: 4.09:1
Front suspension: . . . . . . .Independent with unequal-length A-arms,
  coil springs, tubular shock absorbers, and antiroll bar
Frame: . . . . .Welded tubular steel, ladder type

General

Wheelbase, mm/inches: 2700/106.3
Track, front, mm/inches: 1470/57.9
  rear, mm/inches: 1500/59
Brakes: . . . . .Disc
Tire size, front and rear: 215/70 VR-15
Wheels: . . . . .Cromadora alloy
Body builder: . . . . .Pininfarina

Chapter 28

400 GT and 400 Automatic 1976-85

(Note: Ferrari never produced a 400 GT for the U.S. market. Any example found here has been "Federalized" by one of several private companies who performed this type of conversion. Most of these companies no longer exist. Many of these cars will no longer comply with current emission regulations in many states. Check carefully before you buy.)

Those who thought Ferrari had deserted the sports and GT markets when he added power steering and air conditioning as standard equipment on some models were really in for a shock when the 1976 Paris show previewed a Ferrari equipped with an automatic transmission.

The car is basically the same as the previous 365 GT4 2+2, with the engine enlarged to 4823 cc. It came in two versions: the 400GT, with a five-speed manually shifted transmission; and the 400 A, with a turbo Hydramatic three-speed automatic transmission.

The transmission was furnished by General Motors, and recalibrated to fit the torque characteristics of the V-12. The five speed manual was made by Ferrari.

Pininfarina had also done further work to add comfort and convenience to the interior - redesigned seats, for example. The front seats slid forward on their tracks when the seatback was tilted forward (to allow more room for backseat passengers to get in or out) and were of a new shape that gave more comfort. A quadraphonic stereo system was made a part of the radio/tape system.

Outside, a small spoiler was now incorporated into the lower part of the front end, the taillights were redesigned, a remote-control outside mirror was attached to the driver's door, and the Cromadora wheels were now attached by five lug nuts instead of the center-lock knock-off hubs used before.

Neither this, nor the previous version, was made for U.S. sales, because Ferrari had decided to concentrate on the V-8 as his "Americanized" Ferrari—and it's a pity. Unfortunately, it wasn't in Ferrari's best interests to build them for the very limited U.S. market.

You could buy a 365 GT4 2+2 in Europe and run it through one of the U.S. shops that legalize imported cars, but it would cost nearly $100,000 by the time it was certified. You'd have a great car, though, even compared to Ferraris or other exotic cars.

While Walter Mitty might imagine himself (in one of the earlier Ferraris) as Taruffi in the Mille Miglia, or Gendebien in the Tour de France, there is no mistaking the Rodeo Drive or Park Avenue feeling of the 400 GT or 400 A. The historic V-12 engine sound is there—muffled by insulation and, if converted to U.S. specs, by emission equipment—but the luxurious interior with its air conditioning and stereo sound system leave no doubt about the purpose of this model.

The available power and the excellent suspension will allow high-speed touring in great comfort and with a feeling (real) of safety, but it isn't the Ferrari of old that asked to be driven hard on a winding road while chasing or being chased by Porsches and Cobras.

It is a Ferrari for those of us who now put creature comforts and style ahead of power and speed, without really sacrificing all of the latter.

In 1985, the 412 replaced the 400 GT which, in turn, had replaced the 365 GT4. The "412" derives from the cubic capacity of one cylinder; i.e., 412cc x 12 = 4942 cc (the numbers are approximate, and rounded off—by Ferrari). The modest displacement increase, up from 4823 cc, was accomplished by increasing the bore and stroke by one millimeter, to 82x78 millimeter.

Additionally, the four Weber carburetors were replaced by Bosch K-Jetronic mechanical fuel injection, and a Marelli Microplex electronic ignition was added. The compression ratio was also upped from 8.8 to 9.6:1, and the result was 340 horsepower at 6000 rpm, and 332.7 foot-pounds of torque at 4200 rpm. Drive was transmitted through a 9.5 inch

twin-disc clutch and five-speed all-synchromesh or GM three-speed automatic transmission to the rear limited-slip differential.

Suspension was fully independent, with self-leveling rear shock absorbers, and a Bosch ABS anti-lock system operated on four-wheel ventilated-disc brakes. Top speed for the automatic-equipped car was 152.2 miles per hour, with a standing-start quarter mile in 15.2 seconds; top for the manual-transmission car was rated at 155.3 with a standing-start quarter mile at 14.6 seconds. (It's all quite academic for the U.S. buyer inasmuch as the car was built only for the European market.)

Inside, the headrests (also fitted to the rear seats now) were redesigned, safety belts were repositioned, and the air conditioning/ventilation system had a new electronic control.

The bumpers were color-matched to the body paint, and the foglamps were incorporated into the front spoiler. At the back, the rear deck was raised to improve aerodynamics and increase luggage capacity.

The interior, like the mechanical components, is very reminiscent of the 365 GTC/4, but the 400 has room for two genuine seats in the back. Slight differences can be noted between the manual-shift 365 and the 400 Automatic interiors. Pininfarina

400 GT and 400 Automatic

Engine

Type: ....Colombo-designed, 60-degree V-12
Bore x stroke, mm/inches: 81x77/3.19x3.05
Displacement, cc/cubic inches: 4823/294.2
Valve operation: ....Double overhead camshaft on each bank with cups and spacers operating directly on inclined valves
Compression ratio: 8.8:1
Carburetion: ....Six Weber twin-choke, sidedraft
Bhp (Mfr) ....340 @ 6500

Chassis & drivetrain

Clutch: ....*Single dry-plate
Transmission: ....*Five-speed, all-synchromesh, direct drive in fourth
Rear suspension: ....Independent with unequal-length A-arms, coil springs, tubular shock absorbers, and antiroll bar
Axle ratio: *4.30:1
Front suspension: ....Independent with unequal-length A-arms, coil springs, tubular shock absorbers, and antiroll bar
Frame: ....Welded tubular steel

General

Wheelbase, mm/inches: 2700/106.3
Track, front, mm/inches: 1470/57.9
     rear, mm/inches: 1500/59
Brakes: ....Disc
Tire size, front and rear: ....215/70 -15
Wheels: ....Cromadora alloy
Body builder: ....Pininfarina

*400 A has GM Turbo 400 three-speed automatic and 3.25:1 axle ratio

Introduced in 1976, the 400 GT and 400 Automatic shared the same mechanical and body configura-tion as the 365 GT4, but now with a small spoiler and bolt-on star-design alloy wheels. *Pininfarina*

Little difference can readily be seen between the 365 GT 2+2, 400 GT, and 412, but the quickest identification is the 412's bumpers keyed to the body color and the higher rear deck. *Ferrari*

412

Engine

Type: . . . . Colombo-designed, 60-degree V-12
Bore x stroke, mm/inches: 82x78/3.23x3.07
Displacement, cc/cubic inches: 4942/302
Valve operation: . . . . . .Double overhead camshafts on each bank, with cups and spacers operating directly on inclined valves
Compression ratio: 9.6:1
Carburetion: . . . . .Bosch K-Jetronic fuel injection
Bhp (Mfr) . . . . .340 @ 6000

Chassis & drivetrain

Clutch: . . . .*Double-disc dry-plate
Transmission: . . . . .Five-speed, all-synchromesh, direct drive in fourth*
Rear suspension: . . . . .Independent with unequal-length A-arms, coil springs, tubular shock absorbers with self-leveling system, and antiroll bar
Axle ratio: *4.30:1
Front suspension: . . . . .Independent with unequal-length A-arms, coil springs, tubular shock absorbers, and anti-roll bar
Frame: . . . . .Welded tubular steel

General

Wheelbase, mm/inches: 2700/106.3
Track, front, mm/inches: 1480/58.3
rear, mm/inches: 1500/59
Brakes: . . . . .Bosch ABS with ventilated disc
Tire size, front and rear: . . . . .240/55 VR-16 or 240/55 VR-415 TRX
Wheels: . . . . .Cast alloy 180 TR 415
Body builder and designer: . . . . .Pininfarina
*412 has GM Turbo 400 three-speed automatic and 3.25:1 axle ratio.

Chapter 29

206 and 246 GT Dino 1967-74

On the Pininfarina stand at the 1965 Paris auto show appeared a vehicle labeled Dino 206 S Speciale. Its engine was a Ferrari design; double-overhead-camshaft V-6 with sixty-five degrees between the cylinder banks, and the engine mounted just behind the driver. It was a styling exercise built on a racing chassis (serial number 0834). The engine was a facade, with no internal working parts.

A year later, at the Turin show, a working prototype appeared, called the Dino Berlinetta GT. This was a running automobile but was not to be a production car—yet. Exactly a year later, at Turin again, the car that was to become the 246 Dino GT was shown for the first time. It retained the V-6 dohc engine, but the engine was mounted transversely just ahead of the rear axle.

At this point, the engine was still a two-liter V-6 which was built by Fiat and installed in the Ferrari-designed chassis. Scaglietti was responsible for the construction (Farina design, again) after the chassis was received from Ferrari and the engine from Fiat. The car was called a Dino, and there was no Ferrari emblem or nameplate anywhere on the car.

The vast majority of 206 Dinos, about one hundred in all, were sold in Europe. The 246 version was announced early in 1969, but went into production at the end of 1969. These are the cars you'll most likely find in the United States.

Visually, the 206/246 Dinos remained pretty much the same throughout the model run; but in 1970 the center-lock knock-off hubs gave way to the five bolt wheels, and in 1972 a GTS body style (with removable roof panel, which stowed behind the seats over the passenger compartment) was introduced.

If you intend to purchase a 206 or 246 Dino, one of the first things you should do is have a competent mechanic check the tension of the two timing chains on the forward bank of cylinders (remember this is a transverse-mounted engine). It has been all too common for lazy mechanics to overlook the necessary retenesioning of the chain during service, with the result that a chain will occasionally stretch to the point where it jumps a tooth on the sprocket. This can be disastrous to the valves in the forward cylinder head.

These are quick, maneuverable cars which are enjoyable to drive. They don't have the brute power or marvelous sounds of the V-12 Ferraris, but on a tight, winding road situation they are the match for almost anything on wheels, because their inherent balance makes up for a lack of horsepower.

The Dino is also an excellent car for city driving, because of its light steering and quick response to control input, but the driver's vision is not good to the sides or rear.

The fact that Dinos were not advertised or sold as Ferraris does not detract from their value as an enthusiast's car. They were sold by Ferrari dealers, and I doubt that the lack of a Ferrari emblem or nameplate kept salesmen from calling them Ferraris. You'll surely pay Ferrari prices to get work done on a 246 Dino, but there are fewer parts to buy.

The Fiat in the Ferrari Dino V-6 engine, mounted transversely, just forward of the rear axle assembly, is built mainly by Fiat; except for the lower section (containing oil sump, transmission, differential, and drive shafts) which is built by Ferrari. *Road & Track*

The Dino 206 GT was first shown in 1967 and was produced for European sale. Few found their way to the United States. No 206 or 246 Dino carried a Ferrari nameplate, and it wasn't until the 308 Dino that the series was given Ferrari insignia. This was one of the prototypes. *Pininfarina*

The Dino 246 GT was a 1969 replacement for the 206 Dino. The car shown is a Series I model with the knock-off hubs, which were phased out early in 1970. The 246 was a considerable mechanical evolution. *Pininfarina*

The instruments are different, but the panel layout of the 206 Dino is identical to the Daytona. *Road & Track*

246GT and GTS Dino

Engine

Type: . . . . .Rocchi-designed, 65-degree V-6
Bore x stroke, mm/inches: 92.5x60.0/3.64x2.36
Displacement, cc/cubic inches: .2418/145
Valve operation: . . . . . .Double overhead camshafts on each bank, with cups and spacers operating directly on inclined valves
Compression ratio: 9.0:1
Carburetion: . . . . .Three Weber twin-choke, downdraft
Bhp (Mfr) . . . . .175 @ 7000

Chassis & drivetrain

Clutch: . . . . .Single dry-plate
Transmission: . . . . .Five-speed, all-synchromesh, all-indirect
Rear suspension: . . . . . . .Independent with unequal-length A-arms, coil springs, tubular shock absorbers with self-leveling system, and antiroll bar
Axle ratio: 3.62:1
Front suspension: . . . . . . .Independent with unequal-length A-arms, coil springs, tubular shock absorbers, and antiroll bar
Frame: . . . . .Welded tubular steel

General

Wheelbase, mm/inches: 2336/92.1
Track, front, mm/inches: 1427/56.2
rear, mm/inches: 1430/56.3
Brakes: . . . . .Disc
Tire size, front and rear: .205/70 VR-14
Wheels: . . . . .Cromadora alloy
Body builder: . . . . .Scaglietti (Pininfarina design)

The 246 GTS Dino was introduced in 1972. It shared the mechanical specifications and basic body of the GTB, but notable differences can be seen in the tops. All the U.S. 246s were GTs.

Chapter 30

308 GT4 1973-79

The Paris Salon of 1973 was, as had happened so many times before, the occasion of a Ferrari debut. And, again, there were some firsts for the make. The new car had a transverse-mounted, double-overhead-camshaft V-8 just ahead of the rear axle, and the bodywork was by Bertone. This was the first non-Farina-designed Ferrari GT production car in nearly twenty years.

The new car was designed as a 2+2, even though it didn't carry that designation in its specification. And it had a Dino insignia on the front with no Ferrari prancing horse emblem in evidence anywhere.

Bertone's task was difficult. Designing a 2+2 with a mid-engine has to be a tremendous challenge. The styling of the 308 GT4 hasn't won large acclaim, but considering the design problems, the solution is quite good.

All independent suspension was used with unequal-length A-arms and coil springs, and ventilated disc brakes were now the standard Ferrari equipment.

The engine had ninety degrees between cylinder banks, four Weber downdraft carburetors and, with 8.8:1 compression ratio, produced 205 horsepower at 7700 rpm. Unlike the 246 Dino, the engine was produced entirely by Ferrari.

The Bertone bodywork continued basically unchanged, but in late 1976, the Ferrari prancing horse appeared on the nose, the wheel hubs, and the steering wheel center. Fiat, in control of Ferrari production cars, believed the GT4 would sell better as a Ferrari than as a Fiat.

In view of the varied engine configurations used by Ferrari since 1947—inline four and six, 60-, 65- and 120-degree V-6, V-8, V-12, flat eight and flat twelve—the 246 Dino should have been called a Ferrari. The Dino name was being continued as a tribute to Enzo Ferrari's late son Alfredo "Dino" Ferrari, who has been given credit for instigating the V-6 engined competition cars that also bear his name.

The 308 GT4 is not a luxurious 2+2 because of its limited space, but like many 2+2s before it, is quite satisfactory for short, around-town use for four persons. It would only be suitable for travel for two plus luggage, however.

Because the 308 GT4 was never as popular as the two-passenger models of various types, it is still a relatively good buy. It is the least expensive Ferrari available.

The Dino 308 GT4 was first shown at the Paris salon in 1973 and established a number of firsts for Ferrari; his first mid-engined 2+2 (and a V-8, mounted transversely, at that), and his first production car with bodywork by Bertone. *Bertone*

Although designed as a 2+2, this example is set up for 2+luggage. *Bertone*

The Dino 308 V-8 engine was built entirely by Ferrari and broke new ground by having toothed-belt driven camshafts, rather than chains, which drive the cams on all Ferrari V- 12s (the flat twelve engines shared the toothed-belt-drive system). As in the 246, the 308 Dino is mounted transversely just ahead of the rear axle. *Ferrari*

---

308 GT4

Engine

Type: . . . . .Rocchi-designed, 90-degree V-8
Bore x stroke, mm/inches: 81x71/3.19x2.79
Displacement, cc/cubic inches: 2927/179
Valve operation: . . . . .Double overhead camshafts on each
   bank, with cups and spacers operating directly on inclined valves
Compression ratio: 8.8:1
Carburetion: . . . . .Four Weber twin-choke, downdraft
Bhp (Mfr) . . . .*205 @ 6600

Chassis & drivetrain

Clutch: . . . . .Single dry-plate
Transmission: . . . . .Five-speed, all-synchromesh, all-indirect
Rear suspension: . . . . .Independent with unequal-length
   A-arms, coil springs, tubular shock absorbers with self-leveling
   system, and antiroll bar

Axle ratio: 3.71:1
Front suspension: . . . . .Independent with unequal-length
   A-arms, coil springs, tubular shock absorbers, and antiroll bar
Frame: . . . . .Welded tubular steel

General

Wheelbase, mm/inches: 2550/100.4
Track, front, mm/inches: 1460/57.5
rear, mm/inches: 1460/57.5
Brakes: . . . . .Disc
Tire size, front and rear: 205/70 VR-14
Wheels: . . . . .Cromadora alloy
Body builder: . . . . .Bertone
*One factory brochure lists 205 @ 6600, but another brochure says 240 @ 6600. Both list the European GT4 at 255 bhp.

Bertone's dash is simple and stark; this one with a
180 miles per hour speedometer. *Ferrari*

Chapter 31

308 GTB and GTS 1975-83
308 Quattrovalvole 1983-85
328 Quattrovalvole 1985-89

At the Paris Salon in October 1975, there was (again) a new Ferrari making its public debut. This was a sleek, two-place, mid-engine design by (again) Pininfarina. When the 308 GTB went into production, it was (again) made by Scaglietti.

Utilizing the best design features of the 246 Dino and the 365 GT BB, the new 308 GTB was a handsome styling exercise destined to be *the* Ferrari of the eighties—for the U.S. market, at least.

The first 308 GTB bodies were part metal but mostly fiberglass, the first such use of this material for a Ferrari road car (some of the single-seat racing cars had used fiberglass), but subsequent production models were all metal. Even though the fiberglass was of excellent finish, Ferrari customers could not adjust to "their" car in plastic.

The four-cam, 90-degree V-8 engine was mounted transversely just ahead of the rear axle. Camshaft drive was by toothed belts and carburetion was by four twin-choke, downdraft Webers. Engine output was rated at 205 bhp at 7700 rpm and final drive was through a five-speed transmission.

Suspension was all independent, with the now-familiar unequal-length A-arms front and rear, with coil springs and disc brakes all around. Wheels were Cromadora alloy with five-bolt attachment.

In 1977, an open version, the 308 GTS, was shown at the Frankfurt show. The GTS was a Targa-type spyder with only the small section over the seats being removable. The roof panel stowed behind the seats when removed. Both the open and closed cars carried the Ferrari prancing horse emblems and were officially Ferrari Dinos, rather than simply Dinos, as were the 246s.

Old Ferrari hands decry the descent from a V-12 to a V-8 for power, but the 308 is a Ferrari through and through, regardless of the sounds from the exhaust.

In fact, when the *first* "Dino" V-8-engined car was shown by Ferrari at the 1973 Paris show, it was displayed in 3.0-liter form for export, but concurrently a 2.0-liter V-8 (the 208) was produced for the Italian home market (to circumvent high vehicle taxes based on engine displacement). The car's 1,990 cc engine saw service both in the Bertone-bodied 2+2 and as the 208 GTB.

In 1981, the 308 received Bosch K-Jetronic injection to replace the four dual-Weber carburetors, and the car became known as the 308GTBi or GTSi. At the same time, the 2.0-liter 208's horsepower was increased by the addition of a KKK turbocharger to a respectable 211 horsepower at 7000 rpm.

For the U.S. cars, performance is outstanding even without the turbochargers and even with all the emission controls necessary for U.S. sale. And handling is exemplary. Controls are stiff at low speeds but get lighter as speed increases, the brakes are excellent, and the driver always feels completely in control. The shift gate is notchy, but positive, and the clutch/throttle interplay is easily learned.

308/328 Quattrovalvole

In 1982, the 308 engine was further improved with the installation of four-valve-per-cylinder heads; this version was called Quattrovalvole. In this form, the 2,927 cc engine developed 230 horsepower at 6800 rpm (up from the previous version's 205 at 6600).

All 308 engines got a 2.0 millimeter bore increase and a 2.6 millimeter longer stroke in 1985, bringing the displacement up to 3,185 cc. With this change came a new car designation: 328GTB or 328GTS. Horsepower and torque went up to 260 at 7000 and 213 at 5500, respectively. Bosch K-Jetronic injection was still used, but the ignition was changed from Marelli Digiplex to Multiplex, which Ferrari claimed was more versatile and would control more functions. These specifications remained in effect until sales ended in early 1989.

The evolution under the rear deck made the 308/328 a better car, with quicker acceleration, a higher top speed, and greater flexibility. Literally dozens of mechanical and functional changes, improvements, and upgrades were accomplished. In fact, there were 1,400 changes to the interior alone between the 1985 308s and the 1986 328s!

By 1988, even as the 328's successor—the 348—was nearing production start up, the factory continued to update and improve the current product. Early cars ran on five-spoke wheels that were slightly concave. The 1988 and later cars had convex wheels because the suspension uprights, wishbones, and shock absorbers were changed to improve road ride and comfort while also improving handling.

The last 328 Quattrovalvoles—those produced at the end of model year 1989—used Bilstein shock absorbers. Ferrari introduced its anti-lock braking system (ABS) on the last six months of production. (Many enthusiasts think that the convex wheel designates an ABS car, but this is not true.)

The 308 and 328 series are cars to be enjoyed. Like the Testarossa on *Miami Vice*, the regular television appearance of Tom Selleck's Ferrari on *Magnum P.I.* set the stage very well. Still, the car is not necessarily one in which to travel cross country. Luggage space is minimal, with room for a bit in front contoured around the spare tire and some space behind the engine for larger pieces. This latter area, however, gets very warm.

A small price to pay when you're fighting crime on the big island.

Full complement of instruments and lights, including warnings for catalytic converters getting too hot, face the driver in the small and crowded instrument cluster. *Batchelor*

135

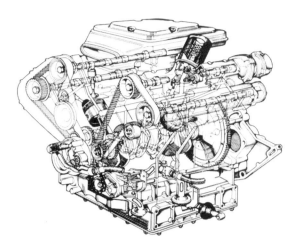

Cutaway of the Dino 90-degree V-8 shows the location of major pieces and the toothed-belt cam-drive system. *Ferrari*

Getting in or out of a 308 requires a certain amount of personal flexibility; but once seated, it's obvious that the car was designed for enthusiast drivers. Panel under right side of dash covers the fuse panels. *Batchelor*

Engine access is not the best and luggage is placed behind the engine, under a zippered cover, and it is not suggested that you carry anything in this compartment that would be affected by engine heat (chocolate bars, for example). *Batchelor*

Paris once again hosted, in 1975, the debut of an important Ferrari model, the Dino 308 GTB. The first series of cars has fiberglass bodies, but later models were all metal. In both cases, the bodywork was by Scaglietti to Pininfarina design. *Ferrari*

In 1977, the GTS joined the ranks, sharing the GTB's bodywork but with black louvers covering the glass behind the doors, and a removable top section that stowed behind the seats. The look has remained the same and this car is a 1981 308 GTSi. *Batchelor*

The 308 Quattrovalvole was almost identical to the
older 308, but could be identified by the roof spoiler
and raised letters on the rear panel. *Ferrari*

138

The 328 shared the chassis and body of the 308, but with the roof spoiler, louvers in the front hood (between the headlights), and bumpers integrated into the underbody fairing and painted to match the body color. *Ferrari*

---

308 GTB and GTS

Engine
Type: . . . . .Rocchi-designed, 90-degree V-8
Bore x stroke, mm/inches: 81x71/3.19x2.79
Displacement, cc/cubic inches: .2927/179
Valve operation: . . . . .Double overhead camshafts on each
    bank, with cups and spacers operating directly on inclined valves
Compression ratio: 8.8:1
Carburetion: . . . . .Four Weber twin-choke, downdraft
Bhp (Mfr) . . . .*205 @ 6600
Chassis & drivetrain
Clutch: . . . . .Single dry-plate
Transmission: . . . . .Five-speed, all-synchromesh, all-indirect
Rear suspension: . . . . . . .Independent with unequal-length A-arms,
    coil springs, tubular shock absorbers with self-leveling system,
    and antiroll bar
Axle ratio: 4.06
Front suspension: . . . . . . .Independent with unequal-length A-arms,
    coil springs, tubular shock absorbers, and antiroll bar
Frame: . . . . .Welded tubular steel
General
Wheelbase, mm/inches: .2340/92.1
Track, front, mm/inches: .1460/57.5
    rear, mm/inches: 1460/57.5
Brakes: . . . . .Disc
Tire size, front and rear: 205/70 VR-14
Wheels: . . . . .Cromadora alloy
Body builder: . . . . .Scagliette (Pininfarina design)
*Bosch K-Jetronic fuel injection for 1981 (308 GTBi & 308 GTSi).
Factory brochures list horsepower variously as 205 or 240.

---

328 GTB and GTS Quattrovalvole

Engine
Type: . . . . .Rocchi-designed, 90-degree V-8
Bore x stroke, mm/inches: 83x73.6/3.27x2.90
Displacement, cc/cubic inches: 3185/194.4
Valve operation: . . . . . . .Double overhead camshafts on each bank,
    with cups and spacers operating directly on inclined valves. Four
    valves per cylinder
Compression ratio: 9.2:1
Carburetion: . . . . .Bosch K-Jetronic mechanical fuel injection
Bhp (Mfr) . . . . .260 @ 7000
Chassis & drivetrain
Clutch: . . . . .Single dry-plate
Transmission: . . . . .Five-speed, all-synchromesh, all-indirect
Rear suspension: . . . . .Independent with unequal-length
    A-arms, coil springs, tubular shock absorbers, and antiroll bar
Axle ratio: 3.82:1
Front suspension: . . . . .Independent with unequal-length
    A-arms, coil springs, tubular shock absorbers, and anti-roll bar
Frame: . . . . .Welded tubular steel
General
Wheelbase, mm/inches: .2350/92.5
Track, front, mm/inches: .1475/58.1
    rear, mm/inches: 1465/57.7
Brakes: . . . . .Disc
Tire size, front: . . . . .Goodyear NCT 205/55 VR-16
    rear: . . . . .Goodyear NCT 255/50 VR-16
Wheels: . . . . .Cromadora alloy
Body builder: . . . . .Scaglietti (Pininfarina design)

Chapter 32

Mondial 8 1981–82 ★
Mondial Cabrio 1983–89 ★ 1/2
Mondial t 1989–92 ★ 1/2
Mondial t Cabrio 1989–92 ★★

Mondial 8 1981–82
Mondial Cabrio 1983–89
Mondial t 1989–92
Mondial t Cabrio 1989–92

The latest in a long line of exciting Grand Touring cars from Ferrari made its debut at the Geneva auto show in March 1980: the 2+2 Mondial 8, with Pininfarina bodywork. The Mondial name (pronounced Moan-Dee-Ahl) was used by Ferrari way back in the early fifties for a 2.0-liter, dohc, four-cylinder sports/racing car, also carrying Pininfarina bodywork.

This Mondial has its 3.0-liter V-8 mounted transversely behind the rear seat, as in the Bertone-bodied 308 GT4. The wheelbase has been lengthened by almost 4 inches, and the seats redesigned so passengers have not only more room, but sit on more comfortable seats as well.

In addition to the normal instruments one expects to find in a high-performance GT car, Ferrari has added electronic monitoring for fluid levels, doors ajar, and lights left on. The interior is upholstered in English Connolly leather, and the leather-covered steering wheel is adjustable for height and reach. Air conditioning and central locking for all doors are standard equipment, as are the remote-control outside rearview mirror and the electric radio antenna. An electrically operated sun roof is optional.

308/328 Mondial

Although the car was introduced in March 1980, production began in 1981. No more than seven or eight examples made it to the U.S. in that model year through Ferrari

North America. This was during the height of the "gray market" import period, and customers frequently acted as their own importers and were then faced with finding aftermarket specialists capable of federalizing their cars.

Mondial engine changes paralleled the 308 GTB and GTS, as would be expected. In 1981, Bosch K-Jetronic fuel injection was added, and in late 1982, the engines received the four-valve-per-cylinder heads, making the Mondial also a "Quattrovalvole," with the same power increase to 230 horsepower at 6800 rpm.

In February 1983, Ferrari unveiled to the world its Mondial Cabriolet. Powered by the Quattrovalvole engine, this was Ferrari's first true open car since the Daytona convertibles in 1969. (The 308GTS versions, it will be remembered, were Targa-type open cars, with a "basket handle" body work structure in place behind the passengers once the roof panel was removed.) The Cabriolet, available in the U.S. during the early summer of 1983, as well as the Mondial coupe, continued as 3.0-liter four-valve models into model year 1985 when the 3.2 Mondial coupe and Cabriolet were introduced.

During 1984 and 1985, Ferrari switched from Bosch's K-Jetronic to the new K-Lambda system, resulting in a small power increase to 240 horsepower. The K-Lambda cars are easily recognizable *audibly* because the idle speed rises and falls slightly as the system adjusts to inputs from the oxygen sensor. (The cars up through model year 1983 had a smog pump; this was eliminated thereafter.)

In 1985, the Mondial engine got a 2 millimeter bore increase and 2.6 millimeter longer stroke, increasing overall engine displacement to 3,185 cc—hence the new designation, Mondial 3.2. Horsepower and torque paralleled the 328 models, with 260 horsepower at 7000 rpm and 213 foot-pounds torque at 5500. Ignition also changed from the Marelli Digiplex to the new Multiplex system.

The Mondial has to be one of the most technically innovative models to come from the Ferrari/Pininfarina collaborations. As a 2+2 with a transversely-mounted engine behind the passenger compartment, it has proven to be more than just a novelty—as shown by its market acceptance. Especially in the Cabriolet form, its popularity among buyers with small families provided its owners with the best of several worlds.

Comfort features expected by American customers have been available in the Mondial since its 1980 introduction, but with the increased power and flexibility of this larger four-valve engine, it became a car seemingly built for the U.S. market. It is able to trundle around town with little regard to gear choice, yet it will go like hell when you're out of town and want to enjoy the performance. The Mondial is improved much more than it would first appear.

Mondial t

As with so many Ferrari models before it, a new version of the Mondial was presented at the Geneva auto show in 1989. The model designation is still Mondial, but followed by a lower-case "t" (for "trasversale") which indicates that the transmission is mounted transversely.

The first Mondials had the mid-mounted engine placed in a transverse position as did the 246 and 308 series Dino Ferraris, but new-generation Ferraris have their engines fitted in the longitudinal position whether front- or mid-engined.

Normally this would necessitate chassis lengthening to accommodate engines longer than they are wide. But the engineers adapted a transmission for the Mondial (and the 348 TB and TS to come) that was devised for the Grand Prix cars at the end of 1974.

Ferrari is among a small handful of companies where it can truly be said that racing improves the breed. The new transverse-mounted transaxle was developed for the 3.0-liter twelve-cylinder Formula One cars (312T) to decrease the amount of weight suspended behind the rear axle—weight that would work like a pendulum to effect handling negatively. To make this transaxle work, the engine crankshaft drives straight into the gearbox via a primary shaft to the flywheel at the back of the transaxle case that is mounted backwards (that is, the flywheel's contact surfaces are actually facing forward; the clutch is *between* the engine and the flywheel). Power from the flywheel is transmitted around the primary shaft by a coaxial shaft forward to a drop gear that drives the bevel gears that turn the power 90 degrees to turn the transmission and rear tires. If it sounds complicated, imagine inventing it and getting it to work.

Mondial 8

Engine

Type: . . . . .Rocchi-designed, 90-degree V-8
Bore x stroke, mm/inches: 81x71/3.19x2.79
Displacement, cc/cubic inches: .2927/179
Valve operation: . . . . .Double overhead camshafts on each bank, with cups and spacers operating directly on inclined valves
Compression ratio: 8.8:1
Carburetion: . . . . .Bosch K-Jetronic fuel injection
Bhp (Mfr) . . . .*205 @ 6600

Chassis & drivetrain

Clutch: . . . . .Single dry-plate
Transmission: . . . . .Five-speed, all-synchromesh, all-indirect
Rear suspension: . . . . .Independent with unequal-length A-arms, coil springs, tubular shock absorbers with self-leveling system, and antiroll bar
Axle ratio: 4.06:1
Front suspension: . . . . .Independent with unequal-length A-arms, coil springs, tubular shock absorbers, and antiroll bar
Frame: . . . . .Welded tubular steel

General

Wheelbase, mm/inches: 2650/104.2
Track, front, mm/inches: 1495/58.9
rear, mm/inches: 1517/59.8
Brakes: . . . . .Disc
Tire size, front and rear: .240/55 VR-390
Wheels: . . . . .Cromadora alloy
Body builder: . . . . .Pininfarina

*Bosch K-Jetronic fuel injection for 1981 (308 GTBi & 308 GTSi). Factory brochures list horsepower variously as 205 or 240.

The 3.2 Mondial was basically like its 308 predecessor. But with color-keyed bumpers completely integrated into the body and the traditional Ferrari egg-crate grille moved up into the bumper from below, it was a more cohesive design. The interior was more luxurious and state-of-the-art comfort features abounded, making it more practical as well as having better performance. *Ferrari*

Pininfarina's design of the new Mondial 8 was first seen at the 1980 Geneva auto show. Production was scheduled to start in 1981. *Pininfarina*

Simple 3.2 Mondial dash with kilometers — therefore, likely European specifications — speedometer. Everything is electronic or electrical now. *Ferrari*

And it works well. The "drop gears" reduce engine revs in the same way the differential ring-and-pinion gears reduce drive shaft revolutions to usable rear axle speeds. And its biggest advantage in road cars is that it allows the engine to be positioned longitudinally with the transmission behind it rather than with the transmission below the engine as is the case of the Boxer and 512s. The center of gravity is lowered, further improving handling. Furthermore, this transmission permitted the engineers to accomplish all this without lengthening the wheelbase.

The Mondial t looks so much like the previous models that it is difficult to tell them apart. It was offered in coupe form in the U.S. in 1989 only, but cabrios continued into model year 1992 when distribution for the U.S. was discontinued. Engine displacement was 3,405 cc, compression was 10.4:1, and horsepower was 300 at 7000 rpm. Top speed of the cabriolet was quoted as 158 miles per hour.

The "t chassis" also received some major revision. Anti-lock brakes were standard, and Bilstein gas-filled shocks automatically controlled suspension stiffness and ride height, though the driver could adjust a cockpit control for soft, medium, or hard. Steering was power assisted.

Body changes were minor but were definite improvements. There was an obvious Ferrari grille in front now and the fender flares were removed. Pininfarina designed the original Mondial and it was responsible for the updates. The "t" cars were the best of the Mondial series—mechanically and visually—especially in the rare Valeo version; it may yet become a significant Ferrari.

For model year 1992, Ferrari produced a double handful of cars known as the "Valeo" Mondials. Valeo is a French clutch manufacturer that produced a system with no clutch pedal but whose clutch was operated by an electro-mechanical actuator

(ECM). This Valeo system can engage and disengage the clutch in 0.02 seconds! Originated for the Lancia rally team, this clutch allowed the drivers to use one foot on the brake and the other on the gas at all times, and it contributed greatly to Lancia's back-to-back world rally championships.

The ECM operated like a manual transmission: Lift off the gas, move the gear shift lever by hand, get back down on the gas, and the clutching was handled without footwork. If you look in the footwell and see no clutch pedal, this is a "Valeo" car. The system is capable of picture-perfect burnout standing launches and even full-throttle shifts. But beware! The module that controls it has a memory, and when you take your worn out Valeo in for service, the mechanics can read the history of your driving style. According to insiders, the Valeo was extremely trouble-free. It was available in coupes as well as cabriolets in Europe, but as only the cabriolets were sold in the U.S., that is how you'll find them here. With its reliability and its rarity—fewer than 30 were imported in 1992—it is destined for desirability.

Mondial t

Engine

Type: . . . . .Ferrari-designed, 90-degree V-8
Bore x stroke, mm/inches: 85x75/3.35x2.95
Displacement, cc/cubic inches: 3405/207.7
Valve operation: . . . . .Double overhead camshafts on each bank, with cups and spacers operating directly on inclined valves, four valves per cylinder
Compression ratio: 10.4:1
Carburetion: . . . . .Bosch Motronic M2.5 fuel injection
Bhp (Mfr) . . . . .296 DIN @ 7200

Chassis & drivetrain

Clutch: . . . .
Twin dry-plate
Transmission: . . . . .Five-speed, traverse-mounted, all-synchromesh, all-indirect
Rear suspension: . . . . .Independent with unequal-length A-arms, coil springs, tubular shock absorbers, and antiroll bar
Front suspension: . . . . .Independent with unequal-length A-arms, coil springs, tubular shock absorbers, and antiroll bar
Frame: . . . . .Welded tubular steel

General

Wheelbase, mm/inches: 2650/104.2
Track, front, mm/inches: 1495/58.9
rear, mm/inches: 1517/59.8
Brakes: . . . . .Anti-lock four-wheel disc, ABSDisc
Tire size, front: .205/55 ZR, 16/225 ZR 16
Wheels: . . . . .Cromadora alloy
Body builder: . . . . .Pininfarina

Last offered in model year 1992, the Mondial t Cabriolet offered the benefits of Ferrari's new "trasversale" transversely-mounted transmission.

This transaxle, developed for the 312T Formula 1 race cars, greatly improved handling for the road cars as well. By 1992, appearance improved as well with bumpers that were, at last, *in* the body rather than *on* it. *Ferrari*

Chapter 33

288 GTO 1984 only

At first glance, the new GTO looked like a modified 308/328, but on closer examination it looked more like what it was: a completely redesigned 308/328. Immediately noticeable were the "flag" outside mirrors, fender flares, larger front and rear spoilers, and four driving lights at the outer ends of the grille.

Not so noticeable was the wheelbase increase of 4.3 inches, to 96.5 inches. This was necessitated by the installation of the engine in a longitudinal position instead of transversely, as in the 308/328. It was still a four-valve-per cylinder, four overhead camshaft V-8, but of 2855 cc (174 cubic inches) displacement, with twin IHI turbochargers blowing through intercoolers into a Weber-Marelli injection system.

In this form the engine, which had originally been developed for Lancia rally cars, developed 400 horsepower at 7000 rpm, and 366 foot-pounds of torque at 3800. This was sufficient to propel the car to almost 190 miles per hour in fifth gear, and gave it a standing-start quarter mile time of 14.1 seconds at 113 miles per hour.

The object of the exercise was to build a FISA Group B competition car, which required a minimum of 200 examples to qualify for the class. In fact, 274 were produced and sold. No plans were made to produce additional cars. None were destined for the American market, although a number found their way to U.S. shores through gray market importers and individuals willing to undertake the expense to federalize them.

As delivered, the GTO was a completely equipped road car, but the owner could add an $1,800 package (to the $83,400 sticker price), which included air conditioning, AM/FM radio and cassette, and electric window lifts.

The new GTO was the first road/competition car built by Ferrari since the original GTO series in 1962, 1963, and 1964. Phil Hill, who knows a thing or two about Ferraris and competition driving, pronounced it a worthy successor to the original.

The GTO looked much like the 308, on which it was based, but had a much larger rear spoiler, larger out-side rearview mirrors, different wheels, and a not-so-noticeable extra 4.3 inches of wheelbase. *Ferrari*

GTO

Engine

Type: 90-degree V-8
Bore x stroke, mm/inches: 80x71/3.15x2.80
Displacement, cc/cubic inches: 2855/174
Valve operation: . . . . .Double overhead camshafts on each
    bank, with cups and spacers operating directly on inclined
    valves. Four valves per cylinder
Compression ratio: 7.6:1
Carburetion: . . . . . . .Weber-Marelli fuel injection, twin turbochargers
Bhp (Mfr) . . . . .400@7000

Chassis & drivetrain

Clutch: . . . . .Twin-disc dry-plate
Transmission: . . . . .Five-speed, all-synchromesh, all-indirect
Rear suspension: . . . . .Independent with unequal-length
    A-arms, coil springs, tubular shock absorbers, and antiroll bar
Axle ratio: 2.90:1
Front suspension: . . . . .Independent with unequal-length
    A-arms, coil springs, tubular shock absorbers and anti-roll bar
Frame: . . . . .Welded tubular steel, fiberglass and Kevlar composite

General

Wheelbase, mm/inches: 2451/96.5
Track, front, mm/inches: 1560/61.4
    rear, mm/inches:. 1562/61.5
Brakes: . . . . .Ventilated disc
Tire size, front and rear: . . . . .Goodyear Eagle VR50,225/50VR-16
Wheels: . . . . .Modular cast-alloy, 16x8 front, 16x10 rear
Body builder: . . . . .Scaglietti (Pininfarina design)

Chapter 34

F40 1987-92

To celebrate forty years of Ferrari automobile manufacture and to honor Il Commendatore Enzo Ferrari himself, the engineers proposed the creation of the "ultimate" Ferrari to be designated the F40. The engineers first proposal was for a fully-equipped road car in the spirit of the recent 288 GTO. It would have a good interior with plenty of luxury. When their proposals reached Ferrari, however, he expressed a desire for a real race car that would be street legal. It would be an honest successor to the 250 GT SWB or the 275 GTB/C, a car for the end of the 1980s like the earlier cars that could be driven to the track, raced, and then driven home.

And so the F40 berlinetta was a barely disguised racing car that can, in fact, be driven on the road. That drive is a thrill but it isn't easy. The twin-disc clutch is stiff (very stiff), the rack-and-pinion steering is not power assisted, and the side windows do not roll down, instead small panels in the middle slide rearward.

The brakes rotors are huge (almost 13 inches in diameter—the same size used in FIA Group C cars) aluminum castings with cast-iron braking surfaces. Four-piston aluminum calipers grab and hold but without the benefit of ABS. Racers, it was argued, could better modulate the pedal pressure themselves and they distrust some electronic brain. Rear vision is also Group C-car-like—negligible at best. The interior is finished in untrimmed carbon fiber composite, its grain pattern apparent everywhere you look and touch. There is no radio, though it couldn't be heard over the engine, tire, and wind noise (and it must be presumed that F40 owners never need to listen to commuter traffic reports). The interior noise level is high enough to make conversation practically impossible. In short, it's an absolutely wonderful, breathtaking automobile that pays back in pleasure and excitement what it demands of its drivers and passengers in sacrifice and tolerance.

What the F40 owner gets is a 2,936 cc, four-cam, four-valve-per-cylinder V-8 with twin sequential turbochargers putting out 478 horsepower in European spec at 7000 rpm and 425 foot-pounds torque at 4000. It's a superb-handling road car that weighs about 2,680 pounds with its 32-gallon fuel tank full. The factory quotes a top speed of 203.4 miles per hour. The 0-to-125 miles per hour times are just 12.5 seconds, and 60 miles per hour comes in just a third of that.

Its Kevlar and carbon composite body is bonded to a steel tube space frame and the all-independent suspension is typical late-model Ferrari with a pair of unequal-length A-arms, coil spring and tubular shock absorbers at each corner, all of it tied together with anti-roll bars front and rear. Road cars were delivered with rubber suspension bushings while the few competition versions were delivered with solid ones.

First available in 1987, it took two years and nearly $11 million to U.S.-certify the cars.

Early cars had no catalytic converters, but by the time of U.S. approval, many European countries had begun to require cats as well so all cars from model year 1989 had them. U.S. cars could not use the rubber fuel cell fitted to European cars because the rubber sweats hydrocarbons, making it nearly impossible for Ferrari to pass the brutally difficult EPA cold-start test. For the U.S., Ferrari fitted an aluminum fuel tank protected that within a second box. These changes plus the addition of side impact protection and federalized front and rear bumpers added about 100 pounds to the U.S. cars. However, in meeting the fifty-state emissions standards on the F40, the catalyst-equipped engines actually made closer to 500 horsepower than 478 because of all the work done for certification. A great deal of the engine management technology came from the Formula One engines.

Around 1,350 of the cars were produced during its five-year life and of those, slightly more than 200 were imported to the U.S. Introduced at $280,000, there are countless stories of early buyers paying from $400,000 to as much as $1.2 million for an F40. This car arrived near the end of the speculator-investor era, a period that made up with money what it lacked in judgment. Good examples of F40s are available now—ten years after introduction and half a decade after it left production—for slightly more than its original list price.

The F40 was Enzo Ferrari's own interpretation of what he and his company represented. While it was available with air conditioning—its only option—it was not a quiet, comfortable, nor luxurious automobile. But the F40 was not about any of those things. It was about racing, the thing that brought Enzo Ferrari to automobiles from the beginning.

For those who couldn't race against Ayrton Senna, Alain Prost, or Nigel Mansell at the time when this car was introduced, or who didn't have the opportunity to fly a jet fighter off an aircraft carrier catapult or land the Space Shuttle, the F40 is for them. It is the ultimate thrill ride for the land-bound enthusiast. On this E-ticket ride, the E stands for Enzo.

With its unabashed race-car looks and its astonishing performance and sound, the F40 became a production dream car. Speculators drove up prices wildly to as much as five times suggested retail. In 1996, good examples can be found for slightly more than the factory recommended new price.

The rear view is the image most non-F40 owners got. Introduced in the U.S. in the days when 55 miles per hour was the legal limit, the F40 reached the maximum national limit in first gear in less than 3.5 seconds. In the mid-nineties, as speed limits increased (or disappeared in Montana), more F40s owners may take advantage and give this view to more drivers.

348 Spider, Speciale

Ferrari enthusiasts (and probably Ferrari's competitors) may wonder how Ferrari and Pininfarina can keep introducing innovative and pace-setting models year after year. Over the years, Ferrari has taken the occasional licking from Porsche, Jaguar, Mercedes-Benz, or Maserati. But no other company has a record of continuous successes to match Ferrari.

The 348, in coupe (tb, for transverse transmission berlinetta) and semi-convertible (ts, for transverse transmission spyder), was introduced at the 1989 Frankfurt auto show. Based roughly on the 308/328/GT, this model used the 3,405 cc 90-degree V-8 engine with twin overhead camshafts and four valves per cylinder. Horsepower was rated at 300 at 7200 rpm. Electronic management was by a Bosch Motronic M2.5 system which controlled each bank of cylinders separately.

Similar to the Mondial, the engine was mounted longitudinally between the driver and the rear axle and drove a five-speed transverse transaxle. In this transaxle, the flywheel was mounted at the extreme rear of the car, ahead of the clutch. Drive then went forward and was turned 90 degrees via nearly identical size bevel gears.

The chassis blended traditional tube-frame technology with a lattice type subframe system at the rear—taken from Ferrari's racing cars—to support the engine and transaxle. The fuel tank was in the center and water and oil radiators were mounted at the sides in order to concentrate the weight toward the car's center. The front suspension was redesigned with anti-dive geometry, and pressed-steel suspension arms reduced unsprung weight. Aluminum brake calipers also helped reduce unsprung weight. The 300 millimeter diameter front discs and 305 millimeter rears were assisted by an anti-lock braking system produced by Ate.

Pininfarina had once again come up with a spectacular body design and shape, borrowing from its own 308/328/GTO and taking several cues from the Testarossa. Wheelbase of the 348, like that of the GTO, is 96.5 inches, but Pininfarina managed to give the 348 a stubby, more aggressive look than it created for the more graceful GTO. Pop-up lights use compound lenses with halogen bulbs. The cheese-slicer side panels are borrowed from the Testarossa, but the remainder of the 348 is unique. The front grille is reminiscent of some of the fifties and sixties models such as the 375 MM, the 196 P, and the 275 LM.

In 1992, Ferrari introduced its Speciale, in production for only one year. The edition was limited to 100 cars, each sequentially numbered and badged to tell its owner where it stood in the sequence run. The Speciale boasted 310 horsepower, due mostly to a more efficient and sporting exhaust system. A lower-ratio, drop-gear set improved the 0-to-60 miles per hour time. The main differences between Speciale cars and the standard berlinetta 348tb were in details and cosmetics. In the interior, the seat from the F40 was stan-

The 348 shows heritage from the Testarossa, and its real predecessor, the 308/328, but even with a four-inch-longer wheelbase (96.5 and 92.5 inches) which it shares with the GTO, the stubby rear overhang gives it a chunky, bulkier look than seen on the 308-328 series. *Ferrari*

Ferrari 348

Engine

Type: . . . . .Ferrari-designed, 90-degree V8

Bore x stroke, mm/inches: 85x75/3.35x2.95

Displacement, cc/cubic inches: 3405/207.7

Valve operation: . . . . .Double overhead camshafts on each bank, with cups and spacers operating directly on inclined valves. Four valves per cylinder

Compression ratio: 10.4:1

Carburetion: . . . . .Bosch Motronic M2.5 fuel injection

Bhp (Mfr) . . . . .300 DIN @7200

Chassis & drivetrain

Transmission: . . . . .Five-speed, transverse-mounted, all-synchromesh, all-indirect

Rear suspension: . . . . .Independent with unequal-length A-arms, coil springs, tubular shock absorbers, and anti-roll bar

Axle ratio: . . . . :1

Front suspension: . . . . .Independent with unequal-length A-arms, coil springs, tubular shock absorbers, and antiroll bar

Frame: . . . . .Unit body/frame

General

Wheelbase, mm/inches: 2450/96.5

Track, front, mm/inches: 1502/59.1

rear, mm/inches: 1578/62.1

Brakes: . . . . .Ate four-wheel disc, ABS

Tire size, front: . . . . .Bridgestone RE71215/50ZR-17

rear: . . . . .Bridgestone RE71255/45ZR-17

Wheels: . . . . .Cromadora alloy

Body builder: .Scaglietti, Pininfarina design

When Ferrari introduced its 348 Spider, it said, "The Spider is for the serious driver who wants to experience the aggressiveness of Ferrari Performance and precise handling in an open cockpit environment." Chassis, tire, and engine improvements over the 328 made the 348s a very much better handling and performing car.

dard in cloth trimmed in leather. An optional "frau" (yes, German for "woman" or "Mrs.") seat put slightly more padding into the F40 composite seat frame. Most buyers ordered a pair of the standard 348 seats because the F40 competition-type seats were too difficult for graceful entry and exit.

Many of the improvements over the standard 348tb that were incorporated into the Speciale were carried over into the Spider introduced in February 1993. In recognition of the importance the U.S. market has played in Ferrari's fortunes, the world debut of the full convertible model was on Rodeo Drive in Beverly Hills, California. When the production versions arrived in May 1993, all were designated as 1994 model year cars.

A sizzling performer, the Spiders were quoted as 171 miles per hour cars with 0-to-60 miles per hour coming in 5.3 seconds. The same drop-gear ratio used in the Speciale was carried over into the 3,252-pound Spider. The 90-degree V-8 produced 310 horsepower at 7200 rpm operating with the Bosch Motronic M2.7 ignition system. Dual electric fuel pumps reside in the bottom of the 23.2-gallon

tank that divides the car full width just behind the cockpit.

Either Bridgestone Expedia or Pirelli P Zero tires were fitted—215/50 ZR 17 at front and 255/45 ZR 17 at the rear—but no spare tire was provided. In fact, a number of potential buyers expressed concern that all Ferrari provided was a can of compressed tire inflation liquid. The factory recommended that the driver consider this an emergency situation and drive no faster than 150 km/h (about 92 miles per hour) straight to get the tire repaired or replaced. Of course, filling the front compartment with even a 50 x 17 series tire and wheel would consume most of the space available. And Ferrari assumed, probably correctly, that 348 Spider owners would be cellular phone-equipped and could simply call in the cavalry when needed. Still, for some owners it limited the possibility of using the car as a daily driver.

The 348's styling was not to everyone's liking, but as with many Pininfarina Ferraris before, it has inspired flatterers to imitate its lines for other car makers. That, of course, is the easy part. Imitating the engine is another matter altogether.

With its longitudinally mounted, 90-degree, 3.4-liter V-8, mated to the trasversale transmission, Ferrari quoted 312 horsepower at 7200 rpm, 0-to-60 miles per hour times of 5.3 seconds and a top speed, top up or down, of 171 miles per hour. A high degree of reliability offered the possibility of using the 348 as a daily driver, but its lack of spare tire (in order to keep some semblance of luggage capacity) made some buyers wary of road trips.

As a future collectible, its value is uncertain because the racers were highly talented amateurs rather than highly recognized professionals. But the 348 Challenge cars provided great entertainment for their owners who raced in a series of events across the U.S. Here Peter Sachs (37) blazes through the last laps of the series opener at Willow Springs in December 1993. As a match-race series, owners purchased their Ferrari 348 Challenge cars, but all maintenance was done by their local dealers who also took responsibility for transportation. It was very close to a kind of fifties-style of gentleman's racing.

Chapter 36

No rating; this model is still in production.

F355 Berlinetta and Spider 1994–

If you liked the 348, you'll love the F355, its replacement. Shown to the world first in mid-1993 at Schwatters, a Ferrari distributor of long standing in Belgium, the car premiered in the U.S. at Monterey in August 1994. Production models arrived before the end of the year.

Some of the excessive styling treatments from the 348—grille work over taillights and the cheese slicer side treatments carried over from the 512s—are gone. In their wake is a Pininfarina design with no muss and little fuss. Ferrari's own literature describes it: "The development goal for aerodynamic characteristics was two fold: negative lift effect without the addition of unnecessary styling elements; a balanced distribution of the front and rear vertical aerodynamic loads on the axles." The side air ducts are generous and merge into the aerodynamically shaped sills which contribute to the wheel fairings required on a car fitted with forty-section tires. The front bumper contains front brake ducts that assist the front spoiler in negating lift.

At the rear, an aerodynamic spoiler, called a "nolder," enhances grip and aerodynamic balance. Some 1,300 hours of wind tunnel work defined the car's shape, clearly reminiscent of the mid-engine V-8s that have come before, but clearly different. And cleaner. What's more, the wind tunnel effort didn't just stop at the rocker panels. The carbon-fiber floor pan is an effective ground-effects surface, even making best use of the

Ferrari F355

Engine
Type: . . . . .Ferrari-designed 90-degree V-8
Bore x stroke, mm/inches: 85x77/3.35x3.03
Displacement cc/cubic inches: 3495/213.3
Valve operation: . . . . .Double overhead camshafts on each bank with unique tapered lateral intake cam valves; three radial intake and two exhaust valves per cylinder
Compression ratio: 11.0:1
Carburetion: . . . . .Bosch Motronic M2.7 fuel injection
Bhp (Ferrari claim): . . . . .375 at 8250 rpm
Chassis & Drivetrain
Transmission: . . . . .Six-speed, transverse-mounted, all-synchromesh, all-indirect
Rear suspension: . . . . . . .Independent with unequal-length A-arms, coil springs, aluminum tubular shock absorbers, and antiroll bar
Front suspension: . . . . . . .Independent with unequal-length A-arms, coil springs, aluminum tubular shock absorbers, and antiroll bar
Frame: . . . . .Unit body/frame
General
Wheelbase, mm/inches: .2450/96.5
Track, front, mm/inches: 1514/59.6
Track, rear, mm/inches: 1615/63.6
Brakes: .Ate four-wheel disc, ABS
Tire size, front: . . . . .225/40 ZR 18
Tire size, rear: . . . . .265/40 ZR 18
Wheels: . . . . .Speedline
Body builder: . . . . .Scaglietti, Pininfarina design

Much of the trim of the 348s disappeared on the F355, and a new, wind tunnel-developed rear end treatment called a "nolder" forcefully enhances rear grip. In fact, some 1,300 hours of wind tunnel work went into devising the shape of the aluminum and steel body and its carbon fiber ground-effects inducing underbody.

air flow past the oil and water radiators by venting them into rear wheelwells where the tires serve as part of the air channels. At the car's top speed, the floor pan and surface aerodynamics combine to produce 220 pounds of down force, according to Ferrari engineers.

In the interior, for the first time, Ferrari offers driver and passenger air bags. Seats are supportive and are normally covered in Connolly leather. However, bucket seats derived from Ferrari racing programs, made of composite materials, are available. The expected gated gearshift lever now handles six forward speeds and its lever will remind drivers of the great silver shifters of the 250 GTO. The suspension is adjustable (for either Sports or Comfort settings) from inside the cockpit. Under the hood, an electronic control unit varies the shock absorbing force within either program on the basis of vehicle speed.

The F355's suspension consists of unequal-length, non-parallel A-arms fitted onto a welded, variable-section steel tube frame plus a tubular sub-frame that supports the mid-mounted engine and rear suspension members. ZF rack-and-pinion power steering is standard equipment. The four-wheel disc brakes use an Ate system that allows the driver to disengage the ABS if desired.

The heart of the car is, of course, the new 90-degree V-8 engine of 213.3 cubic inches with a compression ratio of 11:1. The cylinder block and heads are cast of aluminum alloy with Nikasil cylinder liners. It produces 375 horsepower at 8500

The Spider required an additional 500 hours of wind tunnel time to make its aerodynamics work in either open or closed-car configurations. An active electronic suspension allows the driver to set either "comfort" or "normal" levels. Normal, in Ferrari's book, is for "maximum performance and can be used with a sporty style of driving."

rpm. The dual overhead cams operate five valves per cylinder—three radial intake plus two exhaust valves. The valves use hydraulic adjusters—a first in a car engine capable of revving as high as 8500 rpm. Ignition comes from the Bosch Motronic 2.7 system. The transverse transmission with six-speeds is driven through a single-plate 9.75-inch dry-plate clutch. The engine weighs 370 pounds of the total dry weight of 2,976 pounds.

Overall, the car is 167.3 inches long, rides on a 96.5-inch wheelbase (same as the F40 and 288 GTO) and is shod with 225/40 ZR18 tires in front and 265/40 ZR18s at the rear mounted on magnesium wheels. Ferrari quotes 0-to-60 miles per hour times of 4.6 seconds and a top speed of 183 miles per hour.

Introduced with the F355 Berlinetta was the F355 Spider, "addressed to those 'Ferraristi' who loved the 166 Barchetta, the 250 California, the 275, the 330, the 365, the Daytona, the recent 348 Spider and do not want to renounce driving at the open air." The translation may be a little rough but the intent is clear. Pininfarina's two-seat Spider is constructed in aluminum and steel, just like the Berlinetta. An extra 500 hours of wind tunnel time was invested in making the Spider as efficient through the air as its closed cousin. What's more, the cloth top mechanism is electronically managed by a control unit that coordinates movement of the seats and side windows with raising or lowering the top.

Both the $120,500 F355 Berlinetta and the Spider are now considered the "standard" Ferraris.

Full creature comforts include driver and passenger air bags, environmentally friendly air conditioning, and a complex electric top that readjusts seats and windows before and after raising or lowering. The F355 boasts 375 horsepower at 8500 rpm.

Chapter 37

No rating; this model is still in production.

456 GT 2+2 1995–

The new 456 GT 2+2 may have filled a niche that only Ferrari noticed was vacant. With the probable exception of the Mondial (never labeled a 2+2 as such), 2+2 packages have never sold as well as Ferrari—or some observers—have thought they should. Such seems to be the case right from the start with this truly magnificent grand tourer.

In effect the 456 continues the long line of four-seaters begun first with the 250 GTE 2+2 introduced in Paris in October 1960. The most recent lineage traceable here began with the 1973–76 365 GT4 2+2 that used the 60-degree V-12 with inlets between the cams (from the 365 GTC 4). The 400 GT followed in 1976 with a nearly identical body but with the engine displacement increased to 4.8 liters. Bosch K-Jetronic fuel injection in 1981 caused the car to be renamed the 400i, and slight body changes (a higher rear deck and bumpers color keyed to the body) marked the final evolution to the 412i. This four-seater went out of production in 1986, and for the intervening years, Ferrari had no 2+2 until this new 456. During this decade Enzo Ferrari himself strongly influenced the direction this car would take.

Ferrari's development costs for the 456 were astronomical. And what Pininfarina's designers and Ferrari's engineers produced is nothing short of marvelous—both to look at and to drive. Paul Frere wrote in *Road & Track* that Ferrari had observed even mass-production cars taking advantage of aerody-

Ferrari 456 GT 2+2

Engine:
Type: . . . . .Ferrari-designed 65-degree V-12
Bore x stroke, mm/inches: 88x75/3.46x2.95
Displacement, cc/cubic inches: 5474/334
Valve operation: . . . . .double overhead camshafts on each bank, four inclined valves per cylinder
Compression ratio: 10.6:1
Fuel injection: .Bosch Motronic 2.7
Bhp (Mfr): . . . . .436 @ 6250
Chassis & drivetrain
Transmission: . . . . .Six-speed transaxle, all-synchromesh, all-indirect
Rear suspension: . . . . .Independent with upper and lower unequal length A-arms, electronically controlled shock absorbers, coil springs, antiroll bar, automatic leveling
Axle ratio: 3.64:1
Front suspension: . . . . .Independent with upper and lower unequal length A-arms, electronically controlled shock absorbers, coil springs, antiroll bar
Frame: . . . . .body/frame aluminum/tubular steel unit
General
Wheelbase, mm/inches: 2600/102.4
Track, front, mm/inches: 1585/62.4
Track, rear, mm/inches: 1605/63.2
Brakes: .ATE four-wheel discs, ABS
Tire size, front: . . . . .255/45 ZR 17
Bridgestone Expedia S.01
Tire size rear: . . . . .285/40 ZR 17
Wheels: . . . . .Speedline
Body builder: . . . . .Pininfarina/Pininfarina design

Carrying on Ferrari's tradition of 2+2 coupes begun in 1960, the 1996 model year 456 GT 2+2 carried on another tradition of disappointing sales. Despite attractively aggressive body styling by Pininfarina for this new four-seater, Ferraris—at least in the U.S.—are most desirable as two seaters.

namics to provide more speed than ever before. To Ferrari, that meant his new car must have even more performance—and more traction. Prototypes already running in the late 1980s were scrapped, and the 456 was born with a completely redesigned V-12 engine that was slid rearward in the chassis and mated to a new six-speed transaxle linked by an enclosed driveshaft similar to what was done in the sixties with the 275 and 365 GTBs.

Even Pininfarina's body was put to work on road holding, and the result was not merely low drag. Nearly zero-lift was accomplished by means of a discrete, active flap set into the rear bumper under the back end of the body that provides maximum deflection above 75 miles per hour. The suspension—an electronically controlled derivative of the Bilstein system developed in 1989—offers three variations: sport, intermediate, and touring. Road speed and suspension-impact conditions are constantly monitored, the information is fed back to the shock absorbers to react nearly instantly, automatically shifting the suspension to a firmer mode if the system senses a need. Huge Bridgestone Expedias—255/45 ZR 17 front and 285/40 ZR 17 rears—further serve to keep the car glued to the pavement. The hardware is basically unequal-length, non-parallel arms with coil springs surrounding tube shock absorbers running up the inside of the arms.

Engine management is by Bosch's Motronic M2.7 system. Steering management is done by a ZF Servotronic variable-ratio, speed-sensitive rack-and-pinion arrangement. At extremes of the 2.6-turns lock-to-lock, the steering is 35 percent quicker than in the center. Brakes are Brembo discs with four-piston alu-

Built around a tubular steel chassis, the body is fabricated in light aluminum alloy then spot welded to the chassis through a steel foil interleaf that allows the two-dissimilar metals to be rigidly bonded. The 456 is a big car, 186.2 inches long overall, weighing nearly 4,000 poundwet. Still, Ferrari says it is capable of 186 miles per hour.

minum calipers coupled to the ATE Mark IV anti-lock system.

A new engine, a V-12 of 65 degrees, displaces 334 cubic inches and produces 436 horsepower at 7000 rpm. Compression is 10.6:1. Four valves per cylinder allow the 5.5-liter engine adequate breathing to accomplish 0-to-60 miles per hour times of 5.1 seconds and a top speed of 186 miles per hour, according to Ferrari. Not bad for a car weighing nearly 4,000 pounds at the curb.

The car is so well balanced that driving it gives one the impression of being *inside* a car that is perhaps a third smaller and a third lighter. A remarkable ZF limited slip differential changes from 25 percent locked in traction situations to 45 percent on trailing throttle, the better to keep the back end following the front rather than overtaking it.

The stigma that keeps buyers away from 2+2 Ferraris should be ignored with this car. Its styling is reminiscent of the best of Ferrari's coupes—the back end is plainly an evolved Daytona—and its power and manners, to say nothing of its breeding, bear closer examination. At $207,000 suggested retail price, there are no options. Even the three-piece fitted, pigskin luggage set is included. An automatic transmission is available, introduced in summer 1996.

Mounted in front, longitudinally, is Ferrari's 5.5-liter, 334-cubic-inch, 65-degree V-12, connected by an enclosed propeller shaft to a transaxle gearbox. The fully-independent suspension is electronically adjustable (sport, intermediate, and touring) and it actively adjusts itself to driving style and road conditions.

F50 1995 only

"In the early days of its activity, almost fifty years ago, Ferrari built cars which could be used, with only a few minor alterations, for Formula One or Sport events or for every day use.

"However, as Formula One cars evolved, it became impossible for someone who was not a team driver or a collector capable of passing a series of private tests on a track, to take the wheel of a racing Ferrari. Today Ferrari has decided to give all its clients once again the possibility of experiencing this emotion."

That quote from Ferrari's press material on the startling F50 explained its designation: yes, it was meant to commemorate fifty years of the company and yes, it was the next-step evolution beyond the racing-car-for-the-road F40. But clearly, not all of Ferrari's clients would be able to experience the F50. In all, only 349 were constructed and only fifty-five of those were brought to the U.S.

The F50's chassis was made entirely of Cytec Aerospace carbon fiber and weighed only 225 pounds. With its 27.7-gallon fuel tank filled, the finished car weighed less than 3,000 pounds. Weight distribution was 42 percent front, 58 percent rear. The front and rear suspensions were taken directly from Formula 1 technology. Unequal, non-parallel A-arms link a reaction arm to the electronically controlled Bilstein shock absorbers, surrounded by coil springs and fitted nearly horizontally to immobile points atop the engine and above the front of the cockpit's footwell. Front track is actually wider than the rear, determined by

---

Ferrari F50

Engine

Type: . . . . .Ferrari-designed 65-degree V-12
Bore x stroke, mm/inches: 85x69/3.35x2.72
Displacement, cc/ci: 4700/286.7
Valve operation: . . . . .Double overhead camshafts on each bank. Five valves—three intake, two exhaust—per cylinder
Compression ratio: 11.3:1
Carburetion: . . . . .Bosch Motronic M2.7 system
Bhp (Mfr): . . . . .513 horsepower (SAE) @ 8500 rpm

Chassis & drivetrain

Transmission: . . . . Six-speed, all synchromesh, transaxle
Rear suspension: . . . . . . .Independent, unequal, non-parallel A-arms, push rods connected to Bilstein electronically controlled shock absorbers, coil springs, antiroll bar
Front suspension: . . . . . .Independent, unequal, non-parallel A-arms, push rods connected to Bilstein electronically controlled shock absorbers, coil springs, antiroll bar
Frame: . . . . .Cytec Aerospace carbon fiber tub

General

Wheelbase, mm/inches: 2580/101.6
Track, front, mm/inches: 1620/63.8
Track, rear, mm/inches: 1602/63.1
Brakes: . . . . .Four ventilated discs
Tire size, front and rear: . . . . .245/35 ZR 18; 355/30 ZR 18 Goodyear "Fiorano"
Wheels: Speedline, magnesium alloy, 18x8.5 front; 18x13 rear
Body builder: . . . . .Scaglietti/Pininfarina design

---

engineers to guarantee a tendency for the car to understeer at its limits. The suspension can be set for soft or hard handling.

The transmission is a longitudinally mounted manual six-speed with ZF twin

The body is built entirely of composite material with carbon fiber, aerospace Kevlar, and Nomex honeycomb. The Barchetta version head fairings are anchored to the dual roll bars. If one removes this panel, attaching the Berlinetta roof in its place offers yet another structural element.

cone synchronizers for smoother shifting. It is all housed in a magnesium case. The unassisted rack-and-pinion steering was developed by TRW and is cast entirely in aluminum alloy. Wheel hubs are titanium, the magnesium alloy wheels are built by Speedline and wear special Goodyear "Fiorano" tires developed expressly for the F50. Brakes were designed with Brembo and consist of 14.0-inch-diameter front and 13.2-inch-diameter rear ventilated rotors with four-piston aluminum calipers on each. It is neither power-assisted nor is any anti-lock system used. The engineers developed such a level of smoothness that ABS was deemed unnecessary.

The F50 is powered by a 65-degree V-12 of 286.7 cubic inch displacement (4.7 liters), with 11.3:1 compression. Output is 513 horsepower (SAE) at 8500 rpm. Five valves per cylinder—three intake, two exhaust—are operated by dual overhead camshafts on each bank of six cylinders. Bosch's Motronic 2.7

electronics provide fuel injection and ignition. The crankcase is nodular cast-iron, the connecting rods are titanium alloy, and the pistons are forged aluminum. The dry sump operates with three gallons of oil. The engine's on-board diagnostic system (OBD1) allowed the car to be fully fifty-state legal.

The body was manufactured entirely out of a composite of carbon fiber, Kevlar, and Nomex honeycomb. An integral, removable hardtop made the car both a Berlinetta and a Barchetta. It was offered in only five colors, two of them red, plus yellow, black, and gray. The fully sealed undercarriage formed two venturis, each one exiting the body inside a rear wheelwell. Body styling can best be called Group C for the street. The interior was rather more luxurious than the F40, featuring composite seats (available in either standard size or large!) covered in Connolly leather and a highly breathable insert. Not only were the seats adjustable but so was the foot pedal cluster,

The Berlinetta body (or the open Barchetta) is built around an aerospace carbon fiber tub with attached sub frames for front suspension and mid-engine and rear suspension. The tub weighs only 225 pounds while the entire car weights barely 3,000 pounds wet. It is 176.4 inches long but stands barely 44.1 inches tall.

even to shoe size. The instrument panel was operated by an eight-bit microcomputer, providing 130 elements. Oh yes, and the F50 was air conditioned with a system so efficient as to be effective even as a Barchetta.

Performance was, as expected, as startling as the car's looks. While 0-to-60 arrives in 3.7 seconds, the standing start one-mile comes in 30.3, and terminal velocity is an entirely acceptable 202 miles per hour.

The other startling figure was, of course, its price: $491,000. But none was sold, not a single one. Instead, all were leased for two years. This provided the factory with two benefits. First, it allowed the factory to monitor who got the car, to have the last say. This was done as a way to reward good, long-time, loyal customers. The second benefit was to discourage speculators. The two-year lease price covered a large percentage of the "sticker," leaving only a small buy-back fee at the end. But for any speculator hoping to make a killing selling one at the end of the term, a high price would be defeated by the fact that as many as 349 could come available within a short time. The F50 was not allocated to a dealer, the dealer didn't even buy the car from Ferrari. Dealers only delivered the F50 and collected a commission.

What's it like to drive an F50?

If you owned a 512 and you remembered your learning curve—the amount of time it took you to feel not just confident but comfortable—then multiply that time by four or five. It is that much better, and that much more challenging, an automobile.

This was a no-compromise design collaboration between Ferrari and Pininfarina. Basically a detuned, two-seat Formula 1 car, the front end bears strong resemblance to the legendary 330 P3 and P4 racers. Cooling radiators exhaust heat through large ducting on the front deck.

Seats adjust and so do the foot pedals to provide the driver with the optimum driving position. The foot pads even adjust for the driver's shoe size. The electronic dashboard is rooted in Formula 1 technology and is controlled by an eight-bit computer providing 130 input and output elements.

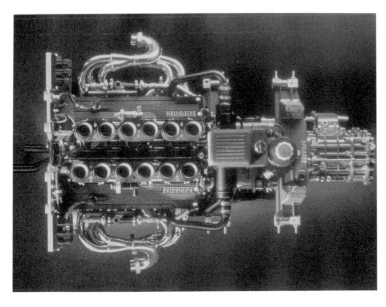

The new 65-degree, 4.7-liter, 286-cubic-inch V-12 uses dual overhead camshafts to operate five valves—three intake radially mounted and two exhaust—per cylinder. Engine output is rated by Ferrari at 513 horsepower SAE at 8500 rpm. The greatest surprise to every first-time rider or driver is the relative quiet of the engine—necessary to meet Switzerland's stringent noise standards. What one hears at speed, however, is glorious.

Chapter 39

The Rare and Exotic

The Ferraris covered in the front part of this book are the ones you'll most likely be able to find for sale. The cars pictured in this section are rare, expensive, and not often for sale. They will not usually be listed in classfied ads but do generally, show up at auctions. Word of the availability of one of these rare gems travels in rather close-knit circles and you have to be "in" to be part of the grapevine.

So how do you get "in"? Join one or all of the Ferrari clubs and get to know the members who already have one or more of the exotics, and subscribe to the *Ferrari Market Letter*. If you're honest about it, and don't make a fool of yourself, sooner or later you'll get firsthand information about a car that you might want. Hopefully, by that time, you'll also be knowledgeable enough (or have several informed friends who can help) to correctly evaluate a car when the opportunity does come. Have money ready; these deals rarely wait.

Buying the right Ferrari can be a marvelous experience, both emotionally and financially. Buying the wrong car can be a disaster. There's no way I can tell you that a certain car is the wrong one; the one that's right for you may be the wrong one for somebody else, and vice versa.

But go to it, you'll enjoy looking, anyway.

Ferrari Grand Prix cars

There was a time when new Ferrari single-seat racing cars were sold to customers to race, and we can remember them appearing in England, Australia, and the United States (for Indianapolis and Pikes Peak). Nobody wanted older models because there was no need or desire for a noncompetitive racing car.

Then we went through a period, starting around the mid-1950s, when no Ferrari single-seaters were available. When a Formula 1 car became obsolete (every year) it was either scrapped, or parted-out and the pieces modified to carry on Ferrari's own racing program. Even established Formula 1 teams couldn't get new Ferraris — in pieces or in complete ready-to-race form.

In the past few years, though, things have changed — at least for older, noncompetitive cars. Several older Formula 1 Ferraris (and a sprinkling of Lotus, Cooper, Maserati, Porsche, and Williams) are seen regularly at vintage car races in the United States and England.

These open-wheeled Ferraris are hard to find and are very expensive when they do turn up for sale. You probably won't find them advertised in magazines or newspapers or at auctions. To learn of the availability of this type of car, one has to be a member of "the grapevine," or have a friend who is (preferably one who won't buy it before he tells you about it).

The prices, though high, are not as high as they could be, because there are fewer collectors who relate to this type of car. There are now vintage racing classes for them.

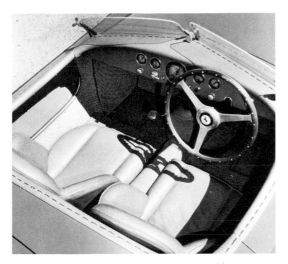

★ ★ ★ ★ ★

The Ferrari that brought attention to the marque in America was the 166 MM (Mille Miglia). Its 2.0-liter Colombo-designed V-12 engine and five-speed transmission were based on Grand Prix Ferraris (even adopting the cylindrical fuel tank from the sin- gle seaters, shown here just ahead of the spare tire). This model was called the "Barchetta," or "little boat." This car, No. 0004M, was built for Luciano Musso in 1949. He raced it in the 1950 Mille Miglia but did not finish. *Batchelor*

★ ★ ★ ★ ★

The 375MM—this one is 0322AM—was a hairy, intimidating competition car. The 4.5-liter Lampredi-designed V-12 produced 340 horsepower, which made the 2,400-pound, Pinin Farina-built aluminum-bodied car a handful for all but the most experienced racers. These competed mostly in long-distance races such as Le Mans and the Carrera Panamericana. This car finished fourth in the Carrera, driven in part by Fabrizio Serena, an executive with Air Italia. This was a 340 model updated with the 4.5-liter engine for the factory team efforts. It set the lap record during the 1953 Le Mans. *Batchelor*

The Michelotti/Vignale combination sometimes produced magnificent shapes, but many times they were over-adorned. This 250 Europa, number 0271EU, is a case in point. Brought into the United States in 1954 by Alfred Ducato, it has remained in original form and looks the same today as it did when new. *Ralph Poole*

★ ★ ★ 1/2
Similar to the 166MM was the 212 Export. The bodywork by Carrozzeria Touring was similar but differences can be seen around the grille and tail-light areas, and there was a two-inch difference in wheelbase — the 212 being longer at 88.6 inches. The car shown is number 0158ED. *Batchelor*

★ ★ ★ ★
One of Michelotti's most interesting designs was built by Vignale on the Ferrari 340 AT (for America Tubolare) chassis. Three coupes (0222AT, 0224AT, and 0226AT) and one roadster (0228AT) were built for the 1952 Carrera Panamericana. The car shown, 0224AT, was driven by Luigi Chinetti to third place behind the Mercedes-Benzes of Kling and Lang. The Ferrari Mexico, as it was called, was at home on long straight stretches of road where top speed could be utilized, but was ill-at-ease on tight, winding roads because of the long wheelbase (102.3 inches) and narrow track (fifty inches). The vertical metal protrusion at the front of each door is a BLAC device (for boundry layer air control) which was supposed to channel air into the rear fender opening to cool the rear brakes. As things worked out, it was more decorative than functional. *Batchelor*

★ ★ ★ ★ 1/2

Carrozzeria Touring stretched the design of the barchetta to fit the 340 America chassis with a 98.5-inch wheelbase. This car, shown with Jack McAfee winning the Palm Springs main event in March 1953, has the long-block Lampredi V-12 engine. *Batchelor*

★ ★ ★ ★ 1/2

Racing and road versions of the 375 MM berlinetta competizione. The bumperless car is of the type driven by Maglioli in the 1953 Carrera Panamericana. *Pininfarina*

★ ★ ★ ★

Probably one of Vignale's best was this 250 MM roadster, number 0260MM, which was Phil Hill's second Ferrari. Phil won Pebble Beach with the car in 1953, was second at Stead Air Force Base, near Reno, won Santa Barbara, but didn't finish at Moffett Field and Golden Gate Park where in both cases the rear axle failed. *Chesebrough*

★ ★ ★ ★

Another rare one; a 166 MM with Vignale body featuring twin windscreens. This car, number 0342MM, was brought into the United States by screen-writer Ranald MacDougall. It is one of the few 166 V-12s with three four-throat Webers — most had two-throat carbs. Randy had rebodied the 166, wrecked it at Willow Springs in 1954, reinstalled the original body, and sold the car. Here it is driven by Jack Brumby at Torrey Pines. *Batchelor*

★ ★ ★ ★

A 250 MM (Mille Miglia) berlinetta was the competition car to own in 1953-54. The three-liter V12 engine was of Colombo origin, but had the individual intake ports and roller cam followers of the Lampredi design and three four-throat Webers. The bodies were by Pinin Farina and all-aluminum. The car shown, number 0340MM, had more than 100,000 road miles on it when sold by Roger Ellis in 1974. *Batchelor*

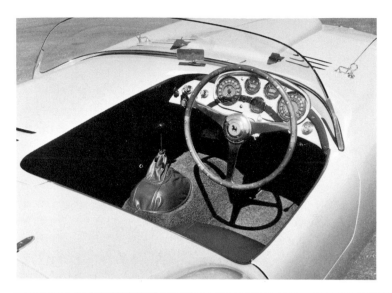

★ ★ ★ ★ ★

This 375 Mille Miglia (No. 0469AM) was purchased new from the factory by Mrs. Willie Day in 1954, and although the car was created as an all-out competition model, it was never raced. Mrs. Day, who resented her husband spending so much money on exotic cars, ordered this one to spite him and specified yellow body paint and yellow-and-green leather. The car remains in the family! *Batchelor*

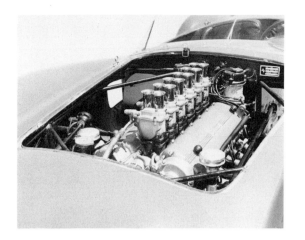

★ ★ ★ ★ ★

This is the 250 TR, or Testa Rossa (red head), with a three-liter V-12 single-overhead-camshaft Colombo-designed engine. The car shown (0756) is a 1958 version with "pontoon" fenders. Later models had smoother body sides, without the protruding nose. The 250 TR was Ferrari's top competition car from 1957 to 1961. *Batchelor*

177

★ ★ ★ ★ 1/2

A very rare car, the 412 MI (Monza/Indianapolis) (No. 0744MI) was a "hot rod" assembled in 1958 for Johnny von Neumann, the Ferrari distributor in California. It combined the chassis of a 250 TR with the four-cam V-12 engine from the 335 Sport which had been built originally for the 1957 Mille Miglia. In 1958, this engine had been installed in a single-seat GT-chassis for the 500-mile race at Monza, Italy, known as the Monzanapolis 500. With this configuration, according to Phil Hill, von Neumann had a car "built to beat the Scarabs." *Batchelor*

★ ★ ★ ★1/2

The Dino 196 S looks like a Testa Rossa and is, in fact, the same basic car with a shortened wheelbase (88.6 instead of 92.5 inches) and a V-6 engine. Some bodies were by Scaglietti, but this car, number 0776TR, has a body by Fantuzzi. The engine is a two-liter, six-cylinder version of the V-12 TR Colombo -designed unit. *Geoff Goddard*

★ ★ ★ ★ ★

This is probably the most coveted Ferrari of all, the 250 GTO. The model was first shown at Ferrari's press conference in February, 1962, and the first car (3223) had no ducktail spoiler on the back. Subsequent cars had a spoiler built into the body, which was built by Scaglietti to a factory design. The GTO has performance, from its 295 bhp V-12 and five-speed gearbox and handsome lines. It is the best possible combination of a road/racing car yet built. Thirty-six 250 GTOs were built in 1962 and 1963, and they are all accounted for. Look in Jess Purret's book *The Ferrari Legend: 250 GT Competition*, but don't expect to find one for less than seven figures in any condition — if you can find an owner who will part with it. The car pictured is number 4293. *Batchelor*

★ ★ ★ ★1/2

The 330 LMB (LeMans Berlinetta) was introduced in March 1963 as a competition car to replace the 250 GTO, and was the last front engined GT car built for competition (the 275 and 365 GTBs were raced, but were built as road cars). The 330 shown is number 4831. *Kurt Miska*

★ ★ ★ ★1/2

A 250 LMB (4713) was built, using a 330 body but with a shorter wheelbase — 94.5 and 98.4 inches. The main distinguishing feature is the more pronounced ducktail on the 250. *Kurt Miska*

★ ★ ★

Ferrari's Formula 1 Grand Prix car in 1955 was the Type 625, powered by a four-cylinder inline twincam engine with 100 millimeter bore and 79.5 millimeter stroke. Power was rated at 260 at 7500 rpm from the 2497.6 cc engine. These old four-bangers are not as exotic as the later sixes, eights, and twelves, but they are nevertheless an important part of Ferrari racing history and, therefore, a desirable car to collectors. *D. M. Woodhouse*

★ ★ ★ ★★

In November 1963, the 250 LM (for Le Mans) was shown at the Paris Salon, and was the first mid-engined GT car from Ferrari that could be driven on the street with any degree, albeit marginal, of comfort. It has a V-12 engine like that of the Testa Rossa, but with 3.3 liters instead of 3.0; as all 250 LMS after the prototype had the larger engine. Ferrari chose to continue calling the model the 250 because he was seeking homologation for GT racing. The car shown is number 6107. *Batchelor*

★ ★ ★1/2

This 312 T2 Formula 1 car was the last of Ferrari's 312 series that began in 1969, all of which were powered by a three-liter dohc flat 12 "boxer" engine. The horsepower rating was 500 at 12,200 rpm and the mid-mounted engine drove through a multidisc clutch to a five-speed transmission in unit with the differential. This 1976 T2 was driven by Nike Lauda part of the season, which helped Ferrari gain the Grand Prix Constructors Championship for l976, but Lauda was injured at the Nurburgring and didn't have a full season of competition. *D. M. Wood-house*

★ ★ ★ ★ ★

Three of these GTO 64s were built. They are basically the same as the fastback berlinetta GTO except for appearance. This is number 5575, the last GTO built. This body design was a great influence on GM designers who created the 1968 Corvette, and it's easy to see why. The lines are functional (other than vision to the rear) and exciting. The car is exceptionally enjoyable to drive, and the investment has to be one of the best. *Kurt Miska*

Serial numbers and numbering system

The first Ferrari sports cars were given three-digit serial numbers that ended with the suffix "C" (for "Corsa"). The "C" was later replaced by "I" (for "Inter"), when "C" became a designation for the Grand Prix cars and stood for *Competitizione*. At that point, in 1948–49, all competition Ferraris had even-numbered designations, while the street/road cars used odd serial numbers. This practice continued until the 312 competition cars, in the mid-sixties, when all Ferraris were given odd serial numbers. To differentiate the Dinos from other models, all models from the 206 through the 308 GT4, were issued even serial numbers. With the advent of the 308 GTB, all Ferraris—Dino, V-8, V-12, or flat-12—were once again given odd numbers, returning to earlier practice.

Early street machines carried three-digit numbers and all the Barchettas ("barchetta" meaning "little boat" in Italian) had even numbers. However, when the 166 Barchetta was introduced in 1949 (as a 166 Mille Miglia with body by Carrozzeria Touring) four-digit numbers were introduced, with the chassis and the engine two numbers apart. This practice began with car number 0051S which was the first road car with a four-digit number. This continued through the first twenty-five cars.

Early Ferraris, with the Colombo V-12 "short" engines, were designated by the following suffixes:
MM=Mille Miglia, 166 or 250

E=Export, 212
EL=Export Lungo, 195
ED or ET =Export Tubolare
S=Sport, 195
I=Inter, 195
EU=Europa
GT=Grand Touring
C=Corsa

Ferraris with the long-block Lampredi V-12 engines carried these suffixes:
AM=America, 340 or 342
AL=America, long chassis
AT=America Tubolare, 340
EU=250 Europa, long chassis
SA=Superamerica, 400, 410, and 500 Superfast

Confusion is likely when researching Ferraris. The factory seems to have used both Export and Sport designations for competition 212s, and the 212 Inter was sometimes called a Europa. Further, serial numbers can't be relied on to establish chronology in the early years. Numbers seem to have been allotted to chassis types, and often cars built months apart will have sequential serial numbers, as though allocated in a book and called upon at the start of each production.

Also, even numbers, reserved at the time for competition cars, sometimes appeared on road cars. Two such examples were the 340 America (0456AM) built by Pinin Farina for Ingrid Bergman in 1954 and 375 MM

(0402AM) built by Scaglietti for Roberto Rossellini in 1955. However, it is possible (probable?) that each was a competition car chassis diverted to road use; they even may have been rebodied competition cars. Given the celebrity status of their owners, many things were possible.

Still another factor that confuses interpretation could be the games Ferrari had to play with the FIA when it was seeking homologation for a new series of Ferraris. For example, the 250 GTOs, built in 1962, 1963, and 1964, were homologated as Grand Touring cars. All carry odd serial numbers, yet the type is essentially a racing car with a roof. But Ferrari intended to sneak this car past the FIA as a "variant" on the 250 GT short-wheelbase berlinetta by calling it an "optional body" on the 250 GT chassis, a chassis that the FIA had already accepted as a production-based racing car (and which carry odd numbers).

The normal location of a Ferrari serial number until the 1970s was on the upper side of the left frame tube, near the front exhaust header pipe. This number should match the number stamped on the identification place attached to the firewall or right inner fender.

The engine number is stamped into the cylinder block on the right side at the back. Beginning in the early seventies, the serial number was also stamped into a plate atop the steering wheel column (so as to be easily visible from outside the car). From 1990 on, the serial number was also placed on the driver's door inner jam.

There were instances in the past where the chassis number may have been covered over, particularly if the frame had been reworked or repainted. In those days, that might have been cause for little concern if you intended only to drive and enjoy the car. But since the surge in both serious- and speculator-interest and prices, obscured serial numbers now should provoke healthy skepticism. There are countless stories of duplicated serial number plates and of number plates being salvaged from totally destroyed automobiles and installed on new recreations. If you're buying the car as an investment, or for show, or if it is a car that is supposed to have a "history," make certain you find those serial numbers. And be sure you confirm their "provenance," that is, their origin. The numbers will be important for the documentation of the car and for future sale.

Model designation

The first Ferraris in 1947 were designated by a numbering system based on the capacity, in cubic centimeters, of one cylinder of the engine. These first Ferraris were called 125s, that is, V-12 engines with 125 cc per cylinder for a total of 1,500 cc displacement.

The number designations were always rounded up, usually to the next highest whole number. For example, the Ferrari 125 actually had 124.7 cc per cylinder. However, the 250 GTO had 246.1 while the 500 Mondial had 496.2. These designations were often only an "accurate approximation."

Thus the 166 Spyder was a 2,000-cc V-12, the 212 Inter was a 2,600-cc V-12, the 340 Mexico was a 4.0-liter V-12, and the 750 Monza was a 3,000-cc inline four. And the 330 GTC was also a 4,000-cc V-12. Most of the time, it was pretty straightforward.

But not always.

When the first Dino was introduced, called the 206, it started a new system of number designations, combining the displacement in *liters* with the number of cylinders. This was meant, as well, to differentiate the mid-engine cars from their front-engined cousins. So the 206 had a 2.0-liter displacement and six cylinders. The 246 Dino was 2.4-liters displacement and six cylinders. However, both cars had V-type engines but, like other Ferrari systems, there is no clue given to engine configuration, only to the size or number of cylinders. The Dino series continued this system through the 308 cars such as the GT4, the 328 cars such as the GTSi (for spider, injected), the 288 GTO (2.8 liter V-8), and the 348 Spider (3.4 liters, V-8).

Logical. Usually. But not always.

The Boxer with its flat-12 began life as a 365 GT4 BB (for Boxer Berlinetta) in 1974 but in 1976 the successor was designated the 512 BB and later, with injection, the 512 BBi. What began as 365 cc per cylinder, evolved into a 5.0-liter twelve-cylinder Boxer. It was replaced by a car simply known as the Testarossa (for "red head," carried over from the 250-cc/cylinder racing cars) introduced in 1985 and subsequently replaced in 1991 by a similar-looking car known as the 512 TR.

But thirty years earlier, the 400 Super America was a 3,967-cc 4.0-liter V-12 engine and 500 Superfast was a 4,962-cc 5.0-liter V-12. These designations were consistent with their times. (Never did the 400SA and 500SF designate horsepower although once that rumor circulated, Ferrari did nothing to correct it.)

But recently, the model numbers got creative. The F40 designated forty *years* and so, one would presume, the F50 represented fifty. However, it arrived in year forty-eight, but, as Ferrari spokepersons explained it, the F50 was the next step in evolution from the F40. Since fifty really would be 1997.

Now to add to the confusion, the F355, as successor to the 348 is, in fact, a 3.5-liter engine, but it's a V-8, not an inline five. And individual cylinder displacement is 436.9 cc, not 355. It's mid-engined. Of course, it has five-valves per cylinder. Hence 355.

And just when everything is confusing, the 456 GT 2+2 arrives with exactly 456.19 cc per cylinder in its V-12 engine. In front.

Got it? Wonderful. Then please explain to a number of frustrated Ferrari researchers what the designations of the 118 and the 121 LM cars of the mid-fifties mean. There will be a quiz on Tuesday.

Ferrari clubs

United States:
Ferrari Club of America
Chris Ahlgrim
P.O. Box 720597
Atlanta, GA 30358
Annual dues $80; some regions have their own dues as well.

Ferrari Owners Club
1-800-57FERRARI
leave message
Annual dues $95

Belgium:
Joseph Cannaerts
Club Ferrari Belgio
c/o Garage Francorchamps
Lozenberg 13,
1932 Zaventem
Belgium

England:
Peter Everinghamn
Ferrari Owners Club
35 Market Place Snettisham
King's Lynn Norfolk
England PE31 7LR

Germany:
Adalbert Lhota
President
Ferrari Club Deutschland
Lyoner Strasse 16
D-60528 Frankfurt am Main
Germany

Hong Kong
T.W.H. Lewis
Ferrari Owners Club
Hong Kong
c/o Italian Motors Ltd.
90 Sung Wong Toi Road
To Kwan Wan, Kowloon
Hong Kong
(fax from U.S.: 011-85-22-530-4184)

Italy:
Sergio Cassano
Ferrari Club Italia
P.O. 589
41100 Modena
Italy

Luxembourg
M. Armand Weyer
Ferrari Club Luxembourg
B.P.2171
L-1021
Luxembourg

Monaco:
Michel Ferry, President
Ferrari Club Monaco
2300 Boullevard Albert Ier
98000
Monaco

Netherlands
T.J.M. Ten hagen
Ferrari Club nederland
Naardenstraat 46 PB 1065
1272 Hulzen
Netherlands

Portugal
J.M.Calen
Club Ferrari Portugal
Rua Da Reboleira 7
4000 Porto
Portugal

Spain:
Club de Amigos Ferrari
Calle Puente Verde 1, 10-3A
Granada, Spain

Switzerland
Tomas Courtin
Ferrari Club Suisse
Postfach 11
7513 Silvaplana
Switzerland

Authorized Ferrari dealers

**North American
Ferrari Dealers**

ARIZONA

Cavallino Classics
7652 East Acoma Dr.
Scottsdale, AZ 85260
602-991-5322 T (telephone)
602-991-5922 F (FAX)

CALIFORNIA

Ferrari of Beverly Hills
9372 Wilshire Blvd.
Beverly Hills, CA 90212
310-275-4400 T
310-246-0400 F

Ferrari of Los Gatos
66 East Main St.
Los Gatos, CA 95032
408-354-4000 T
408-354-3996 F

Ferrari of San Francisco
595 Redwood Highway
Mill Valley, CA 94941
415-380-9700 T
415-380-0365 F

Ogner Motorcars, Inc.
21301 Ventura Blvd.
Woodland Hills, CA 91364
818-884-4411 T
818-884-8747 F

COLORADO

Ferrari of Denver
4300 South Federal
Englewood, CO 80110
303-730-7340 T
303-797-8874 F

CONNECTICUT

Miller Motorcars, Inc.
342 West Putnam Ave.
Greenwich, CT 06830
203-629-3890 T
203-629-1621 F

FLORIDA

Crown Auto Dealerships, Inc.
6001 34th St. N.
St. Petersburg, FL 33714
813-527-5731 T
813-521-4489 F

The Collection
200-240 Bird Road
Coral Gables, FL 33146
305-444-5555 T
305-444-8237 F

Shelton Sports Cars
5750 N. Federal Highway
Ft. Lauderdale, FL 33308
305-493-5211
305-772-2653

GEORGIA

Ferrari of Atlanta
3862 Stephens Court
Tucker, GA 30084
770-939-5464 T
770-939-5344 F

HAWAII

Continental Cars Ltd.
1069 S. Beretania St.
Honolulu, HI 96814
808-537-5365 T
808-545-3203 F

ILLINOIS

Continental Autosports
420 E. Ogden Ave.
Hinsdale, IL 60521
708-655-3535 T
708-655-3541 F

Lake Forest Sports Cars, Ltd.
780 N. Western Ave.
Lake Forest, IL 60045
708-295-6560 T
708-295-8849 F

MASSACHUSETTS

Gaston Andrey of Framingham, Inc.
1800 Worcester Road
Framingham, MA 01701
508-875-0639 T
508-875-3570 F

MISSISSIPPI

Ferrari South, Inc.
419 S. Gallatin St.
Jackson, MS 39023
601-969-5668 T
601-355-1292 F

NORTH CAROLINA

Foreign Cars International
4401 W. Wendover Ave.
Greensboro, NC 27407
910-294-0200 T
910-294-9109 F

NEW YORK

Steven Kessler Motorcars, Inc.
317 E. 34th St.
New York, NY 10016
212-689-0770 T
212-689-2877 F

Wide World of Cars
125 Route 59 E.
Spring Valley, NY 10977
914-425-2600 T
9140425-7387 F

OHIO

Midwestern Auto Group
5016 Post Road
Dublin, OH 43017
614-889-2571 T
614-898-2877 F

OREGON

Ron Tonkin Grand Turismo, Inc.
203 N.E. 122nd Ave.
Portland, OR 97230
503-255-7560 T
503-257-2407 F

PENNSYLVANIA

Algar Ferrari of Pennsylvania
1234 Lancaster Ave.
Rosemont, PA 19010
610-527-1100 T
610-525-0575 F

TEXAS

Ferrari of Dallas
500 N. Central Ave.
Richardson, TX 75080
214-470-9410 T
214-680-0982 F

Ferrari of Houston
6541 Southwest Freeway
Houston, TX 77074
713-772-3868 T
713-772-1472 F

Motor Imports, Inc.
96 N.E. Loop 4410
San Antonio, TX 78216
210-341-2800 T
210-341-5260 F

UTAH

Steve Harris Imports, Ltd.
808 S. Main St.
Salt Lake City, UT 84101
801-521-0340 T
801-521-0673 F

VIRGINIA

Ferrari of Washington
45180 Business Court
Suite 500
Sterling, VA 20166
703-478-3606 T
703-478-3769 F

WASHINGTON

Grand Prix Motors, Ltd.
1401 12th Ave.
Seattle, WA 98122
206-329-7070 T
206-329-7073 F

CANADA

BRITISH COLUMBIA

Carter Motor Car, Ltd.
Luxury Car Division
1770 W. 7th Ave.
Vancouver, BC. V6J 4Y6
604-736-2821 T
604-736-1567 F

QUEBEC

Luigi Sports Cars, Ltd.
6450 Banden Abeele St.
Ville St. Laurent, Quebec
514-336-4449 T
514-336-6882 F

TORONTO

Maranello Sports, Inc.
5243 Steeles Ave.
Toronto, Ontario M9L 2W2
416-749-5325 T
416-749-9780 F

Recommended Ferrari reading

There is a wealth of information in print (and out of print) about Ferrari's road cars and racing efforts. This list comprises a small assortment which the authors have found commendable. Those out-of-print are identified by the abbreviation (OP) after their titles:

Ferrari Omnia Opera & Catalog Raisonne
4 volumes, Edited by Bruno Alfieri

Ferrari: The Early Berlinettas and Competition Coupes
Ferrari: The Early Spiders and Competition Roadsters
Ferrari: The Gran Turismo and Competition Berlinettas
Dean Batchelor

Ferrari Guide to Performance (OP)
Allen Bishop

The Spyder California: A Ferrari of Particular Distinction (OP)
George Carrick

Ferrari Spider
Piero Casucci & Bruno Alfieri

Origins of the Ferrari Legend
Gioachino Colombo

Inside Ferrari
Michael Dregni

Ferrari Testa Rossa V-12 (OP)
Joel Finn

Ferrari: The Sports & Gran Turismo Cars (OP)
4th revised edition
Warren Fitzgerald, Dick Merritt, and Jonathan Thompson

Ferrari: The Man, The Machines (OP)
ed. by Stan Grayson

A Salute to Ferrari
Louis Klementaski & Jesse Alexander

Ferrari —On The Road
Stan Nowak

DINO: The Little Ferrari (OP)
Doug Nye

The Colonel's Ferraris (OP)
Doug Nye

Ferraris at LeMans (OP)
Dominique Pascal

Ferrari Turbos —The Grand Prix Years 1981–1988
Anthony Pritchard

Grand Prix Ferrari (OP)
Anthony Pritchard

The Ferrari Legend: 250 GT Competition (OP)
Jess G. Pourret

Ferrari Sport, Racing and Prototypes Competition Cars (OP)
Antoine Prunet

The Ferrari Legend: The Road Cars
Antoine Prunet

Ferrari Type 166 (OP)
Gianni Rogliatti and Lorenzo Bascarelli

Ferrari (OP)
Hans Tanner & Doug Nye (6th revised edition)

Ferrari Formula 1 Cars 1948–1976
Jonathan Thompson

L'Anteprima Ferrari 815
Franco Varisco

Ferrari Cars 1946–1956
Ferrari Cars 1957–1962
Ferrari Cars 1962–1966
Ferrari Cars 1966–1969
Ferrari Cars 1969–1973
Ferrari Cars 1973–1977
Ferrari 328/348/Mondial 1986/1994
R.M. Clarke, Brooklands Books

Cavallino magazine
Box 810819
Boca Raton, FL 33481-0819

Ferrari World magazine
19 Kensington Court Place
London W8 5BJ

Forza magazine
P.O. Box 1529
Ross, CA 94957-9987

Index